THE GREAT GENERALS SERIES

This distinguished new series will feature the lives of eminent military leaders who changed history in the United States and abroad. Top military historians will write concise but comprehensive biographies including the personal lives, battles, strategies, and legacies of these great generals, with the aim to provide background and insight into today's armies and wars. These books will be of interest to the military history buff, and, thanks to fast paced narratives and references to current affairs, they will be accessible to the general reader.

Patton by Alan Axelrod

Grant by John Mosier

Eisenhower by John Wukovits

LeMay by Barrett Tillman

Omar Bradley by Alan Axelrod

Andrew Jackson by Robert Remini

LeMay

Barrett Tillman

palgrave
macmillan

LeMay
Copyright © Barrett Tillman, 2007.
All rights reserved.

First published in hardcover in 2007 by PALGRAVE MACMILLAN® in
the US—a division of St. Martin's Press LLC, 175 Fifth Avenue, New York,
NY 10010.

Where this book is distributed in the UK, Europe and the rest of the world,
this is by Palgrave Macmillan, a division of Macmillan Publishers Limited,
registered in England, company number 785998, of Houndmills,
Basingstoke, Hampshire RG21 6XS.

Palgrave Macmillan is the global academic imprint of the above companies
and has companies and representatives throughout the world.

Palgrave® and Macmillan® are registered trademarks in the United States,
the United Kingdom, Europe and other countries.

ISBN-13: 978-0-230-61396-6
ISBN-10: 0-230-61396-9

Library of Congress Cataloging-in-Publication Data Tillman, Barrett.
LeMay / Barrett Tillman ; foreword by Wesley K. Clark.
    p.   cm. — (Great generals)
Includes bibliographical references and index.
ISBN 1-4039-7135-8 (alk. paper)
ISBN 0-230-61396-9 (paperback)
  1. LeMay, Curtis E.   2. Generals—United States—Biography.
3. United States. Army—Biography.   4. United States—History,
Military—20th century.   I. Title.   II. Series.
E745.L42T54   2007
358.40092—dc22
[B]

                                                        2006047524

A catalogue record of the book is available from the British Library.

Design by Letra Libre

First PALGRAVE MACMILLAN paperback edition: April 2009
10 9 8 7 6 5 4 3 2 1
Printed in the United States of America.

Contents

Photosection appears between pages 92 and 93

Timeline

November 15, 1906	Born in Columbus, Ohio.
1924	Entered Ohio State.
October 1928	Entered the army as a flying cadet.
October 1929	Commissioned a lieutenant; assigned to Selfridge Field, Michigan.
1934	Assigned to Wheeler Field, Hawaii.
December 1936	Assigned to 2nd Bomb Group in Virginia.
August 1937	Located the target ship *Utah* off the West Coast.
February 1938	Lead navigator on B-17 formation flight to Argentina.
May 1938	Intercepted the Italian liner *Rex* over 600 miles at sea.
December 1939	Lead navigator on formation flight to Brazil.
January 1940	Promoted to captain.
March 1941	Promoted to major, squadron commander in 34th Bomb Group.
January 1942	Promoted to lieutenant colonel.
May 1942	Assumed command of the 305th Bomb Group.
September 1942	Led the 305th to England, began combat operations.
1943	Assumed command of Fourth Bomb Wing (later Third Bomb Division), Eighth Air Force.
August 17, 1943	Led the Regensburg portion of the "double strike" missing including Schweinfurt.
September 1943	Promoted to brigadier general.
March 1944	Promoted to major general.
August 1944	Assumed command of XX Bomber Command in China.
January 1945	Assumed command of XXI Bomber Command in the Marianas.
October 1945	Commander AAF Research and Development.
September 1947	Army Air Force becomes the independent U.S. Air Force.
October 1947	Commander USAFE.
January 1948	Promoted to lieutenant general.

June 1948	Organized the Berlin Air Lift.
October 1948	Assumed command of Strategic Air Command.
Summer 1949	Testified in congressional hearings regarding SAC capabilities in comparison to naval aviation.
September 1949	Soviet Union detonated its first nuclear device.
1951	Promoted to full general.
July 1957	Appointed air force vice chief of staff.
July 1961	Appointed air force chief of staff.
July 1965	Retired.
1968	Ran as George Wallace's vice presidential candidate.
October 1, 1990	Died.

LeMay Airplanes

Consolidated PT-3	Two-seat biplane trainer (first flew 1927).
Curtiss P-1	Single-seat biplane fighter (1925).
Douglas O-2	Three seat biplane observation plane (1923).
Douglas OA-4	Eight-seat, twin-engine monoplane amphibian (1931).
Boeing B-17 Flying Fortress	Ten-man, four-engine bomber (1935).
Consolidated B-24 Liberator	Ten-man, four engine bomber (1939).
Boeing B-29 Superfortress	Eleven-man, four-engine strategic bomber (1942).
Boeing B-50 Superfortress	Improved version of the B-29 (1947).
Consolidated B-36 Peacemaker	Fifteen-man, six-piston, four-jet intercontinental bomber (1946).
Boeing B-47 Stratojet	Three-seat, six-engine jet bomber (1947).
Boeing B-52 Stratofortress	Six-man, eight-engine jet bomber (1952).
Boeing KC-135 Stratotanker	Four-man, four-engine jet tanker (1956).
Convair B-58 Hustler	Three-man, four-engine supersonic jet bomber (1956).
North American XB-70 Valkyrie	Experimental two-man, six-engine Mach Three bomber (1964).

Foreword

NO NAME IS MORE ASSOCIATED WITH AIRPOWER THAN General Curtis LeMay. He flew, built, and led the greatest air force the world has ever known. He fulfilled the most awesome visions of earlier military theorists, creating the airpower force that destroyed Japan, and, ultimately compelled its surrender. Subsequently, he created the force that deterred Soviet aggression and preserved the peace during the Cold War. Barrett Tillman's masterful biography of LeMay brings this critically important military leader to light in the context of his own time and challenges, but also leads the reader to question the most fundamental precepts of airpower itself, and LeMay's role within air force history.

Born in 1906, Curtis LeMay grew up around the country, developed an early love for flying, and, dropping out of university due to lack of funds, joined the National Guard and worked his way into pilot training and a flying slot. It was a demonstration of the determination that so often provides the earliest markings of lifetime achievement. LeMay didn't just want to fly, though—he wanted to master the profession. He learned right away that perhaps the skill most critical for aviation's long term potential was navigation. He studied, practiced, and as a young officer became the Army Air Corps' finest navigator. Later, he demonstrated the same foresight in teaching himself to use the famed Norden bombsight, one of America's most critical pieces of World War II era technology.

In the years before World War II, as LeMay was developing his aviation skills, military thinkers all over the world understood that the stalemate of trench warfare, with its millions of casualties, had to be broken. In the newly-formed Soviet Union, the shrunken but still-potent Reichswehr was conducting secret experiments in deep maneuver using armored formations. British veterans like B. H. Liddle Hart were extolling the value of the Indirect Approach. Airpower visionaries like the Italian Douhet were evoking images of fleets of long range bombers flying far over hostile territory, raining terror from the skies, and Army Air Corps General "Billy" Mitchell was proving that airpower posed a formidable threat to traditional notions of sea power. Curtis LeMay didn't compete in the battle of ideas. Instead, he saw what needed to be done, and he worked to assemble the skills, tools, and later, the people, to do it.

LeMay was a tough taskmaster. He sent men into to combat and knew he would take losses. First in command of a squadron of the new B-17 bombers, then in command of the Fourth Bomb Wing, and later in command of the famed Eighth Air Force in England in 1943 and 1944, he became the youngest Lieutenant General in the war. He perfected massed formation flying, stacking the bombers to maximize their survivability against German fighters, training and designating specially qualified bombardiers, and then organizing the flights to follow their lead. In doing this, he gave the United States its early capabilities for precision daylight attack, going after German industry in specific efforts to break the back of the Nazi war machine. By comparison, the British were reduced, by their losses and their bombers' inaccuracy, to nighttime strikes on population centers.

Transferred to the Pacific theater, LeMay quickly adapted to the new B-29 bomber and a different enemy. First in the China-Burma-India theater, and later in the Western Pacific, LeMay built the necessary training and support systems, and made the crucial targeting decision to firebomb the largely wooden Japanese cities in an effort to end the war. In March, 1945, General LeMay's bomber force attacked Tokyo and other cities from low altitudes with incendiaries. His purpose was to help end the war, as quickly as possible. Huge firestorms were created, and hundreds of thousands of people—largely innocent civilians—were killed. It was brutal. America had adopted the tactics of their British allies. And then, the most momentous acts of all: LeMay's B-29's dropped the first and then the second atom bombs. With this, and with the entry of Russian forces into the war against Japan in China, the war was over.

At the end, only the United States possessed the atomic weapons and the bomber forces necessary to wield airpower on an intercontinental scale. The U.S. Air Force had earned its place as an independent service. And at its heart, there was the newly-named Strategic Air Command. After only a few months, General Curtis LeMay was put in charge. Again he went to work—training, discipline, and readiness were his watchwords, as he molded an intercontinental force first of bombers, and then of bombers and missiles. This was perhaps the most significant military task of the Cold War era, providing the United States with the military means to deter Soviet aggression.

In later duties, as Vice Chief and then Chief of Staff of the United States Air Force, there were other challenges, and other controversies. He fought for his service's needs against the Army and Navy, and, as a member of the Joint Chiefs of Staff, he advised Secretaries of Defense and Presidents on national policy. As a retired officer he dabbled in right-wing politics, even accepting the nomination to run for Vice President on the ticket with Alabama Governor George Wallace.

In retrospect, many have expressed reservations about firebombing cities. Such acts today are outlawed. But LeMay and his bosses believed that the best means to save lives was to end war quickly, and however horrible and regrettable, and whatever private anguish they may have felt, they did what it took. When it came to his military duties, LeMay didn't philosophize, he performed.

Later, saddled with policy responsibilities in an America adrift in the confusing strains of the Cold War, Vietnam, and racial tensions, LeMay found himself in a different arena. His directness, candor, and get-it-done practicality that made him the indispensable commander in war were less useful here, in the grip of powerful political and diplomatic forces.

In the meantime, LeMay's airpower has continued to mature, allowing us to strike with greater precision over ever longer ranges, and to penetrate enemy defense with stealth and many varieties of countermeasures. Airpower alone may not be enough to win every conflict, but American supremacy in this regard has become the bedrock of U.S. national security. Resonating in all this is LeMay's legacy as the architect and practical visionary who took abstract concepts and built the world's greatest air power.

—*General Wesley K. Clark*

Introduction

ON THE AFTERNOON OF MARCH 9, 1945, MAJOR GENERAL Curtis E. LeMay turned from the runway on Guam's North Field and paced back to his waiting vehicle. The thirty-seven-year-old airman had just rolled the professional dice in an all-or-nothing bid to turn the strategic bombing campaign against Japan from a costly experiment into a bold stroke that might end the Second World War.

The tropical air still pulsed with the resounding throb of 1,384 powerful engines carrying 346 Boeing B-29 Superfortresses to burn out the heart of the Japanese Empire. LeMay, who had commanded the world's most powerful bomber force for only six weeks, felt the burden as never before.

As the huge silver "Superforts" tucked their wheels into their wings and left the Mariana Islands behind, they carried more than a mixture of explosive bombs and incendiaries. They bore the institutional hope of the Army Air Forces, their chief in Washington, D.C., and the prayers of thousands of fliers and maintenance personnel who devoutly wished an early end to the world's bloodiest war.

The B-29s also bore the professional future of Curtis LeMay.

When he assumed the leadership of XXI Bomber Command, LeMay had bluntly been told that if he failed he would be fired, though it was far from certain who could replace him. In any case, all his previous success would be ignored.

LeMay fully realized the technical, tactical, and doctrinal risks he was taking. The U.S. Army's heavy bombardment strategy was mated at the hip with the doctrine of high-altitude daylight operations. In vivid contrast to the British Royal Air Force and the German Luftwaffe, the Americans persisted in their belief that precision bombing could be more effective than nocturnal missions against area targets—basically, city-sized objectives.

LeMay had seen the results firsthand. Two years previously, leading his B-17 group from England, he had survived the attrition from German flak and fighters, and raised bombing accuracy to unprecedented levels. Then, running the B-29 campaign from China, he had fought logistics and geography as well as the Japanese in an effort to bring strategic weight against the enemy's home islands.

Now, all that counted for very little. LeMay had replaced an old friend at the helm of XX Bomber Command and was determined not to repeat the doctrinal errors of his predecessor. Winds and weather over Japan conspired to destroy bombing accuracy from high altitude in daylight, so LeMay decided on a vastly different solution.

He had just launched nearly 3,500 fellow airmen on a low-level mission over the enemy capitol, at night. In several hours he would know whether he had helped turn the war around or whether he should pack his bags and prepare to return to the States in disgrace.

Returning to his headquarters, LeMay appeared typically calm and unruffled to his staff. But it was going to be a very long night.

CHAPTER 1

Wings

THE FLIER'S NAME WAS LINCOLN BEACHY, AND HE FLEW through the San Francisco sky in a machine called an aer-o-plane. The twenty-eight-year-old Ohioan was hailed as "the flying fool," drawing thousands of spectators to the Panama-Pacific Exposition. The exposition was the equal of a world's fair, attracting national and international participants of all kinds.

In 1915, one of the witnesses to Beachy's aerial antics was eight-year-old Curtis Emerson LeMay. He had seen an aer-o-plane only once before, but the sight was acid-etched in his memory. Since that defining day in his parents' Ohio garden some five years before, young Curtis had been enthralled with the concept of flight. Seeing an aer-o-plane for the first time, he yearned for "the drive and speed and energy of the creature."[1]

Beachy continued flying as what later generations called a stunt pilot. His usual aerial routine was memorable, but he ended his career in 1915 by plunging into San Francisco Bay, the victim of a structural failure in an untried airplane. An estimated 75,000 people witnessed his fall from 200 feet: at once the high and the low of the exposition. One of LeMay's heroes was gone, but the inspiration gestated, sprouted, and cropped.

+======+

Curtis E. LeMay was born in Columbus, Ohio, on November 15, 1906, twelve months after Erving and Arizona Carpenter LeMay's wedding. His given name was chosen by his mother, who "just drew it out of thin air." Likewise, his middle name was chosen "because she liked the sound of Emerson."[2]

By his own reckoning, Curtis's youth was nomadic. Erving was a steel worker and handyman who moved the family wherever employment beckoned: to Pennsylvania, Montana, California, and back to Ohio in 1919. In that time the family grew with the addition of two more boys and three girls: brothers Leonard and Lloyd, and sisters Methyl, Patricia, and Velma.

Young Curtis displayed his ambition and willingness to work almost from the start. He took a variety of part-time jobs and odd chores, saving money for a bicycle. He recognized the monetary potential in a bike, as it would enable him to increase his earning power with a paper route. Even at that tender age, he was goal oriented and planned for the future.

Among Curtis's early pursuits was the Boy Scouts, in which he accumulated most of the merit badges required for Eagle, the highest scouting rank. However, time was an asset in shortage, and LeMay lacked sufficient opportunity to complete all the requirements. Raised with a serious work ethic, his paper route and other jobs limited the time he could devote to scouting. Consequently, his scouting career peaked at First Class, halfway up the ladder to Eagle.

LeMay's first full-time job was more pleasure than business: At the neighbors' request he shot birds with his BB gun in order to feed their voraciously lazy cat. At a nickel a pop, young Curtis became a deadly marksman. Perhaps unknowingly, at a tender age he absorbed the Clausewitzian lesson of economy of force: maximum effect for minimum expenditure.

Curtis LeMay was what later generations called a self-starter. He received little encouragement from his parents to pursue particular interests, so he developed his own. One was reading, beyond the confines of the classroom. He preferred historical fiction and biography, though travelogues also appealed to him. Wanderlust became a character trait, both personally and professionally.

The boy's social life was, by his own admission, minimal. Dating, what he called "the girl stuff," cost money that could be applied to more immediate pursuits: guns and radios. He had a passion for all manner of machinery, especially engines and electronics. Always skilled with his hands, Curtis saved enough money to buy the components for a crystal radio set and before long he was listening to stations as far afield as Pittsburgh and Cincinnati. He much preferred hunting and mechanics to socializing, and proved an awkward date. Until relatively late in life the female half of the human race took second place to his "happy little tinkerings."[3]

The career of an army pilot held fascination for LeMay, and he was astute enough to realize that a regular commission offered something approaching job security. But the thought of competing for a West Point appointment was too daunting: In 1924 he took the road more traveled, opting for ROTC at Ohio State. He majored in civil engineering and worked night jobs. The two were incompatible. Cadet LeMay, at the top of his military studies, was frequently too tired for many other classes after working a shift in a steel mill to meet tuition. Five hours' sleep per night simply could not sustain an academic lifestyle.

The ROTC instructor was Lieutenant Chester Horn, who imparted a sense of objectivity and balance not always present in

Scabbard and Blade organizations. In averting a tentative feud with campus pacifists, Horn reminded his charges that the world always turns, and eventually both "cowards" and "warmongers" could be proven right—and wrong.

Forced by finances to leave OSU, LeMay demonstrated the persistence that marked his career. Despite his poor academic standing, he gained entry to the Ohio National Guard on basis of his excellent ROTC record and set his sights on becoming an aviation cadet.

In October 1928 LeMay reported to March Field near Riverside, California. Not long afterward he was able to resign his artillery position in the Guard in order to apply as a regular army officer.

LeMay's first aircraft was the Consolidated PT-3, a state-of-the-art trainer, new that year, with a 220-horsepower Wright engine. The instructor and student sat in open cockpits, one behind the other. The PT-3 was rated at an optimistic 102 mph but cruised at 80 and a bit more.

LeMay graduated from pilot training at Kelly Field, Texas, and was commissioned in the Air Corps Reserve October 1929. Four months later, standing in the snow before a Curtiss P-1, LeMay was sworn into the Regular Army Air Corps with fourteen other officers.

The graduates in LeMay's advanced training class comprised an Air Force galaxy studded with stars. Among the 117 newly winged airmen were some historic names: Nathan Bedford Forrest and George B. McClellan, whose grandfathers had fought in the Civil War; Emmett O'Donnell, who slipped to a later class after an accident; Jesse Auton, who would command an Eighth Air Force fighter wing; William H. Tunner, who became "Mr. Airlift," leading the aerial lifelines over the Hump and into Berlin; Laverne G. "Blondie" Saunders, who began World War II at Pearl Harbor and would lead the India B-29 command; and Frank F. Everest, commander of a bomb group in the Pacific during World War II and the Fifth Air Force in Korea.

Lieutenant LeMay's first assignment was the Twenty-seventh Pursuit Squadron at Selfridge Field, Michigan. Ironically, considering that he became a big bomber advocate, he spent most of his first decade in fighters. The Twenty-seventh was a prestige assignment—its origins harkened back a decade to the glory days of Frank Luke, "the Arizona Balloon Buster" who received a posthumous Medal of Honor for his 1918 exploits.

Most new pursuit pilots were delighted to fly fighters: not LeMay. From the beginning he demonstrated a voracious appetite for knowledge and experience beyond immediate duty. His attitude was soon noticed, bringing him an assortment of assignments sometimes beyond his junior status. He took a course in celestial navigation and mastered instrument flying with the rudimental gauges of the period. For a fighter pilot, droning along under the hood of a Douglas O-2 observation plane was only marginally more glamorous than serving as airdrome officer. But LeMay realized that tail chasing and dogfights would not win wars: The ability to penetrate hostile airspace in all weather, day or night, just might. Perhaps without realizing it, Curt LeMay was becoming less a "pursuiter" and more a bombardment man.

In the fall of 1933 LeMay was among a dozen officers sent to a navigation course at Langley Field. The school was run by Harold Gatty, a Tasmanian veteran of the Royal Australian Navy. An accomplished professional, he had guided Wiley Post's round-the-world flight in 1931. The Army Air Corps hired him to establish navigation schools in Virginia and California, and seldom was public money better spent. Previously, aerial navigation largely was done by "pilotage," following visual cues such as railroad tracks or highways. Pilots had seldom used "dead reckoning," or flying by time and estimated distance computed over featureless terrain. But as LeMay said, under Gatty's system, "we entered a new world."[4]

Gatty had applied his nautical experience to aviation, permitting improved celestial and dead reckoning navigation (using only time and speed to estimate distance covered). The timing of his lessons proved fortuitous. With faster, longer-ranged aircraft becoming available, army fliers could benefit from Gatty's techniques. There was "turf" concern in the navy—army pilots seldom ventured far over water—but technology and doctrine were merging. The long-range strategic bomber would soon roll out of the institutional hangar, with the range to cover vast areas of ocean previously the domain of battleships.

LeMay took Gatty's lessons to heart—with a philosophy to match. Recognizing the tremendous potential in all-weather flying, the student eventually became a tutor. He mastered the instrument-flying trade in typical LeMay style: a full-ahead, feet-first entry into the potentially chilling waters of instrument flight. Whenever possible he checked out a Douglas observation plane, flying "under the hood," a cockpit covering permitting no outside view.

Early in 1934 LeMay and his colleagues found themselves the unintended victims of a political vendetta. The new Roosevelt administration, still eagerly dismissing Hoover-appointed Republicans, claimed improprieties in the Hoover administration's issuance of airmail contracts. President Franklin Roosevelt asked the chief of the Air Corps if the army could take over the airmail, and Major General Benjamin Foulois leapt at the chance. After only hours of consultation with the post office department and his own subordinates, Foulois gave a "can do" response. That was all Roosevelt needed. Most existing contracts were cancelled on February 9; the army was to begin flying the mail in ten days. Lieutenant LeMay embarked upon his first dangerous assignment.

Foulois's optimism was wholly misplaced, and a disservice to his men. Though he issued a "safety first" dictate, neither his pilots nor many of his aircraft were up to the challenge. That winter was one of the hardest on record, with arctic temperatures and reduced visibility. Coupled with the fact that most mail was flown at night, army airmen began dying in headline-grabbing numbers. Three were killed just training for the mail flights.

Lieutenant Colonel H. H. Arnold ran the Air Corps' western division from Salt Lake, where the first three fatalities occurred. Even so determined an optimist as Hap Arnold described the situation as "most impossible."[5]

Despite the highly publicized deaths (eight in a few months), LeMay later insisted that the biggest danger was cadging enough money to eat, since no extra funding was provided for the mail flights. In February he began flying between Richmond, Virginia, and Greensboro, North Carolina. Part way through the airmail project LeMay was ordered to Wright Field near Dayton for a "blind landing school," learning to land with reference to instruments. He continued flying the familiar Dougas O-2 biplane but graduated to the new twin-engine Martin B-10 monoplane bomber, a much faster and more complex aircraft.

Widely reported as a fiasco in the press, the army airmail program was cancelled after seventy-eight days. A dozen fliers were killed and fifteen badly injured in sixty-six crashes—nearly one a day. Owing to prudence and unpreparedness, the army completed less than two-thirds of its scheduled flights.

The year 1934 was significant for Curtis LeMay personally as well as professionally. On a blind date, he had met a young lady named Helen Maitland and began courting her. He even swapped assignments with another junior pilot, Lieutenant Robert L. Scott, so both could be nearer their girlfriends. LeMay and Helen were married in Cleveland on June 9. They established officers' quarters at Selfridge Field, where LeMay fought a losing campaign against his wife to keep his new mustache. He concluded that it was a "good idea to let them [brides] have obvious victories every now and then. Helps the morale."[6]

Only weeks after the wedding, LeMay was transferred to the Sixth Pursuit Squadron at Wheeler Field near Honolulu. The slow boat to Hawaii passed through the Panama Canal, and though LeMay was never stationed there, he acquired a lasting memento.

According to Strategic Air Command (SAC) staffers, in Panama he picked up a stubborn virus that settled in his mouth. Eventually he found that tobacco offered temporary relief, leading to his trademark cigar chewing.

The Sixth Pursuit was undermanned, so Lieutenant LeMay was assigned an onerous variety of tasks, including communications, engineering, assistant operations, and mess officer. The smorgasbord of jobs interfered with flying, but in retrospect LeMay saw professional advantage in the diverse tasks, especially in the realms of operations and maintenance.

Among LeMay's other chores was working as a navigation instructor. Working with Lieutenant John W. Egan, LeMay developed a curriculum involving both classroom and flight time. With a variety of castoff aircraft, including Douglas OA-4 amphibian airplanes, the proprietors of "Egan and LeMay's Young Men's Navigational Seminary" admitted that they operated "one jump ahead of the students," but they also produced results. Their more precise methods expanded the Army's traditional overland flying into long-range ocean navigation, and LeMay personally developed a powerful reputation as an over-water navigator. Of the twin-engine Douglases he said, "We flew the damn things to death."[7]

Somewhere along the way, LeMay began pondering the relative merits of pursuit versus bombardment aviation. By their nature, fighters were defensive weapons whereas bombers could carry the war to an enemy's heartland. LeMay remained uncertain whether John Egan planted the seed, but eventually LeMay concluded that pursuit, being defensive, could not win a war. Only the offensive team could do that—and that meant bombers.

When he was promoted to first lieutenant in March 1935, LeMay had been a "second John" for six years. His remaining two years in Hawaii passed pleasantly enough, but LeMay had already decided upon a change. Since he burned his bridge in the 6th Pursuit with a blunt, reasoned analysis of the squadron's poor showing in a war game, he had no qualms about opting out of fighters. When he came up for reassignment he requested transfer to the Second Bomb Group at Langley Field, Virginia.

CHAPTER 2

Bombers

NO SOONER HAD LIEUTENANT LEMAY UNPACKED HIS BAGS at Langley Field than he found himself employed as a navigator rather than a pilot. His record at the Gatty school and his creden tials as an instructor in Hawaii had preceded him. He was expected to organize a navigation school for the Second Bomb Group along the lines of the Hawaiian curriculum. LeMay was appalled: He knew fighters and amphibians well, but next to nothing about bombardment aviation.

Upon reporting to the personnel officer, LeMay sought a way out of his tutorial dilemma. But an old ally was close at hand. John Egan also had papers to the Second Bomb Group, and would arrive in a few months. LeMay reasoned that since his old partner was a bomber man from the ground up, it made sense for Egan to run the Langley school while LeMay learned his new trade. The personnel department accepted his reasoning, and LeMay checked into the Forty-ninth Squadron as assistant operations officer, compiling duty rosters and planning missions.

LeMay's arrival at Langley coincided with delivery of the first Boeing B-17s. Twelve "Y1Bs" were built for service evaluation, identifying and eliminating technical "bugs" such as engine problems and high altitude performance. As with any complex aircraft, there were bound to be growing pains, but for young aviators like LeMay, the big, gleaming Boeings were futuristic marvels.

Today, with their glass framework noses and almost art-deco styling, they may appear quaint. But in 1937 there was nothing like them: huge, gleaming engineering masterpieces of latent power and polished aluminum. Considering that the army was flying mediocre twin-engine types such as the Martin B-10 and Douglas B-18, the big, four-engine Boeings inspired awe and confidence. With their speed, range, and altitude, they were unlike anything then in service.

Curtis LeMay was exactly where he wanted to be.

There was another influence at Langley, far more significant than the B-17. The group commander was Lieutenant Colonel Robert Olds, who made a lifelong impression upon LeMay. Olds was the first man LeMay ever met who "really penetrated my thick skull with a sense of urgency in getting things done. . . . I didn't know what it was all about until I began work under Bob Olds."[1]

Olds was already something of a legend in the Air Corps. A true believer in heavy bombardment, he had been Brigadier General Billy Mitchell's aide during the airpower crusader's much-publicized trial for insubordination in 1925. As war approached, Olds helped draft strategic bombing doctrine by anticipating what the Air Corps would need: more personnel and bases, newer aircraft, and a plan for using them.

Exacting taskmaster that he was, Olds recognized talent when he saw it. Before long LeMay became operations officer for the entire group. Along the way, LeMay absorbed his commander's leadership philosophy: Keep out of people's way once you've told them what you want done. Other components of Olds's philosophy became imprinted as if in LeMay's DNA: thoroughness, precision, and uncompromisingly high standards.

Another important influence upon LeMay was Brigadier General Frank M. Andrews, the first commander of General Headquarters Air Force. A former cavalryman, "Andy" Andrews was a fervent believer in strategic bombardment. With Mitchell's crusading example before him, Andrews incurred the severe displeasure of some superiors in congressional hearings by advocating a quasi-independent air force. He was broken to colonel and sent to ponder his sins in Texas purgatory, but he was not sidelined for long. General George C. Marshall retrieved him for important work in the Mediterranean and Europe during the war.

LeMay's Hawaiian expertise proved of increasing value. Known as an expert at over-water navigation, he was assigned to the Second Bomb Group's joint exercise with the Navy in August 1937, locating the target ship USS *Utah* off the West Coast. When the elderly battleship could not be found, Olds grumbled some suspicions and ignored LeMay's theory that the intended "victim" merely was just in the wrong place. The next day Olds was vindicated when the Navy admitted the quarry was sixty miles from the briefed position. When the target turned up missing a second time, the army men wondered whether the problem truly was accidental. In any case, Olds, LeMay, and the Second Group proved they could find ships in the open ocean and attack them.

As the new bombers were mastered, Olds began seeking ever greater challenges. In 1938 he set back-to-back transcontinental speed records with one of the Boeings: thirteen hours east-west and under eleven on the return. More challenges quickly followed.

Having proven himself an exceptional navigator, LeMay was instrumental in the first "mass" long-range flight for the new B-17s, six planes to Argentina, February 15–27, 1938. Flying with Major Caleb "C. V." Haynes, LeMay was lead navigator, using the only gyro-stabilized drift sight on the mission, providing the most accurate information on wind direction and speed. He enjoyed needling other pilots by recommending impossibly precise headings such as "thirty-one and three-quarters degrees."[2]

The flight went almost flawlessly, showing the American flag during President Ortiz's inauguration. The fliers enjoyed the festive atmosphere of Buenos Aires (LeMay noted, "They keep pretty late hours down there") and the mission was a technical triumph. Consequently, the group received the Mackay Trophy for most significant flight of 1938.

That was a landmark year. In May, a more difficult mission was proposed by Colonel Ira Eaker, the Air Corps' chief of information. This time it was far more than a publicity stunt: the search for a single ship hundreds of miles offshore. If successful, the flight could bring political support for a larger Air Corps and a role in defending America on a par with the navy. Beyond that, it hinted at the fliers' ultimate goal: an independent air force equal with the army and navy.

The goal assigned by Eaker was three B-17s making a pinpoint intercept of the Italian liner *Rex* far off the Atlantic coast. The glamorous cruise ship was scheduled to arrive within 700 miles of New York on May 12, and the Second Group was assigned the task of finding her. To ensure sufficient press coverage, three reporters were invited along, including a radio reporter to provide on-scene commentary. The mission commander was Major Vincent Meloy, while LeMay, as usual, was lead navigator flying with C. V. Haynes.

Everyone assigned to the project recognized the potential benefits in proving long-range army aviation. Likewise, they recognized the colossal pitfall if the bombers failed to find the target. In his memoir, LeMay quipped, at that moment his name might have been spelled "DisMay."[3]

At Mitchel Field on the morning of May 12 Haynes sidled up to LeMay and asked, assuming the *Rex* was on course, what time the bombers would find her.

LeMay recomputed his figures and, with more confidence than he felt, replied, "I make it 12:25."

General Frank Andrews knew what Lieutenant LeMay was experiencing. Just before takeoff time he looked directly at the navigator and said, "Good luck."[4]

The weather refused to cooperate. Clouds and rain squalls forced the Boeings to climb from 600 to 6,000 feet and descend again. Turbulence buffeted the big bombers. Charts, navigation protractors, and coffee mugs levitated; stomachs protested. And time winged onward at 200 mph.

Tracking the wind, LeMay had additional concerns. He confided to Haynes that their groundspeed was ten knots less than expected

Then things got worse. The three Boeings penetrated a cold front while flying line abreast, with heavy rain smacking the airframes. It took ten minutes to punch through, but eventually the bombers burst into bright sunlight. LeMay watched his clock tick down to the appointed moment of sighting the ship, conscious that three impartial observers—one with a live radio link to Mr. and Mrs. America—expected to see the *Rex* at 12:25.

There she was.

The fliers confirmed her identity by the Italian colors on her funnels, and then descended for a low-level pass. The photographers were delighted. So was the *Rex*'s captain, who radioed an invitation to stop in for lunch.

The glorious moment was necessarily short-lived. With fuel an ever-present concern, the Boeings turned for home, but the westbound return through the storm front was worse than the outbound leg, with even greater turbulence.

Still, it was a PR windfall. Among others, the *New York Times* gave the mission extensive coverage, crediting the army men with a pinpoint intercept 610 miles offshore. (Later reports gave the distance as 755 miles.)

Time magazine was so impressed with the mission that it lauded the lead navigator, misidentifying LeMay as First Lieutenant Curtis "Selby."[5]

In August the B-17s returned to South America, visiting Colombia in another goodwill gesture. However, a more serious purpose lay beneath the surface: determining tactical matters such as takeoff intervals, time en route, and high-altitude flight. Crewmen learned more about using oxygen bottles during prolonged cruising above 15,000 feet—crucial knowledge for later combat operations.

In December 1939 seven B-17s, including new production models, flew to Brazil. For diplomatic purposes Major General Delos C. Emmons was nominal commander of the flight, but Olds possessed the technical knowledge and LeMay navigated. The round trip covered nearly 11,000 nautical miles in sixty-three and a half hours flying time for an average groundspeed of 173 knots (199 statute miles per hour). Thanks to the Second Bomb Group, the B-17 was now a known quantity: capable of long-range, high-speed cruising over long distances.

Between all the flying and navigating, LeMay was trying hard to start a family. Helen had two miscarriages but she wanted a child as much as her husband. Finally a daughter, Patricia Jane (Janie), was born in February 1938.

While at Langley, LeMay took it upon himself to master the B-17's Norden bomb sight. It was a sophisticated piece of equipment for its time, among America's greatest military secrets, permitting a high-flying bomber to place ordnance on target from as high as 30,000 feet. LeMay's interest was more academic than practical, as pilots were preoccupied with learning to fly their new planes. However, as a pilot and navigator LeMay believed that a thorough professional should know all the aspects of his trade. He succeeded, being widely regarded as the best pilot, navigator, and bombardier in any unit he joined.

From 1939 onward, existing Army Air Corps (AAC) units were divided and subdivided to provide cadres for new squadrons and groups. The expanded Air Corps relied heavily upon experienced personnel, many of whom were given greater authority and responsibility than their ranks ordinarily obtained.

LeMay was no exception. After eleven years of commissioned service, he finally made captain in January 1940.

Barely a year after making captain, LeMay found himself a temporary major commanding a squadron in the new Thirty-Fourth Bombardment Group. In February 1941 the group was based at Westover Field near Springfield, Massachusetts. Like everything else in that expanding prewar period, the primary condition was chronic shortage: barracks, aircrews, mechanics, and airplanes.

While struggling with human and materiel deficits, LeMay received a call from his former Langley crew commander, C. V. Haynes. With permission from his group commander, LeMay met Haynes in Montreal, where Haynes explained the nascent Atlantic Ferrying Command. Canadians already were recruiting civilian and former military pilots to fly aircraft to Britain. But the ferrying system was often backlogged from too few planes and lack of qualified crews to shuttle ferry pilots and high priority passengers between Canada and Britain.

LeMay was indifferent about becoming essentially an airline pilot, but he definitely liked the people involved. Within arm's reach of C. V. Haynes was Bob Olds, running all of North Atlantic Ferry Command (NAFC).

LeMay also was attracted by NAFC's equipment. The brand-new Consolidated B-24 (not yet named Liberator) was selected as the primary ferrying aircraft, and the veteran B-17 man liked what he saw. The '24 was everything the Boeing was not: boxy and slab-sided, with a long, thin wing. It had more speed and range than the '17, which commended it to the transatlantic route. LeMay qualified in the new bomber with one landing, and then made his first run to Scotland.

The North Atlantic was a weather factory, requiring hours of instrument flying. LeMay's early experience in over-water navigation and his personal regimen of flying under the hood served him extremely well, whether fighting ice over mid ocean or sweating an instrument approach into Gander, Newfoundland, or Prestwick, Scotland.

However, there were other routes to be flown. That September LeMay joined C. V. Haynes in flying Major General George H. Brett's airfield survey team from Brazil to Africa. He was the same Major Brett who had commanded the Twenty-seventh Pursuit Squadron when LeMay arrived at Selfridge Field. But it was not all cheery old times. LeMay and company waited in Egypt and, while Brett's crew went up country, acquired dysentery in the hotel. LeMay lost fifteen pounds in five days. Upon return home, he lurched through the door and eased himself toward bed, as he said, "like a wounded cockroach." The effects lasted three months.[6]

Upon rejoining the Thirty-fourth group at Westover, LeMay was given a new assignment: Group operations officer. It was the position he held on Sunday, December 7, 1941.

Japan's surprise attack stunned LeMay as it did millions of other Americans. His reaction was "a feeling of complete unreality."[7]

However, there was also a sense of relief that the period of tentative anticipation had ended. "Now we knew where we were going," LeMay said. "We were going to war."[8]

CHAPTER 3

England

In January 1942 most of America's Pacific coast lay wide open to attack. Thinking that the Japanese were bound to pursue their stunning victory in Hawaii, the U.S. Army and Navy rushed scarce assets to the far west, bolstering a pitiful state of readiness.

One of the units sent to the Pacific Northwest was the Thirty-fourth Bomb Group, which deployed from New England. LeMay sent Helen and three-year-old Janie to stay in Cleveland until further notice, and then clambered aboard his Liberator.

Toward the end of January the group landed at Pendleton Army Airfield in Northeastern Oregon. LeMay had hardly touched down when he received new orders: A telegram had preceded him, directing him to Wright Field near Dayton, Ohio. His previous transatlantic experience in B-24s had been duly noted, marking him as a

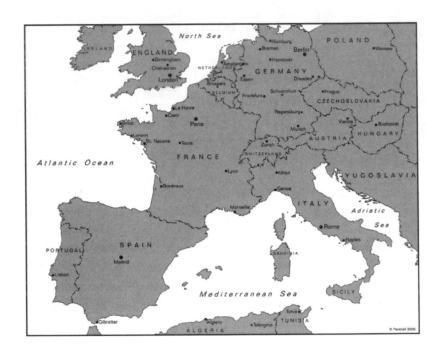

prime candidate to complete the Consolidated bomber's service evaluation. The family was briefly reunited in Ohio before LeMay returned west.

Back in Oregon, he hardly had time to unpack his duffel bag. With new units forming weekly, a pilot of his experience was a plum waiting to be picked. Colonel Charles B. Overacker commanded the 306th Bomb Group at Wendover, Utah, and wanted LeMay as his executive officer, or second in command.

While it was flattering to be requested by name, LeMay balked at what he saw at Wendover—or, more accurately, what he did not see. Built "smack in the middle of the Bonneville Salt Flats," Wendover was one of the most remote, desolate army facilities in the zone of the interior, 130 miles from Salt Lake. LeMay admitted that after the first look, he wanted to take off and fly away.[1]

Eventually LeMay and some other officers established themselves in the State Line Hotel, which straddled the Utah-Nevada border. The LeMay family settled in, and Janie promptly charmed the hotel staff into providing her with candy and Cokes while her father tried to season the half-trained, uncomprehending rookies assigned to the 306th.

The stay at Wendover ended in May when LeMay was sent to Salt Lake to assume command of another new group, the 305th. It had been activated in March, but was hardly more than a paper entry. When LeMay arrived, the group had three B-17s and a monumental need of everything else: men, equipment, and know-how. Curt LeMay began providing what was needed most: leadership.

It was no easy task. The 305th had four squadrons, each of which was short of everything, especially experienced crews. (LeMay was one of three pilots in the group who had ever flown a B-17, recently dubbed the Flying Fortress.) The new group commander quickly learned who could be trusted to get things done. In his memoir, LeMay was effusive in his praise for two former enlisted men, Benjamin Fulkrod and Ralph Cohen.

Fulkrod had been a prewar maintenance chief, commissioned shortly after Pearl Harbor. Reserved and taciturn by nature, LeMay was sparing with superlatives, but Fulkrod's talent may be gauged by the CO's description of him as "a genius" at aircraft maintenance.

Cohen, the armament officer, received equal praise. A former marine, he applied his practical and theoretical knowledge about machine guns to the hundreds of weapons eventually acquired by the 305th.

Russell E. Schleeh was among the early pilots joining the 305th. He recalled years later that LeMay personally supervised "partial-panel" instrument check rides, learning to compensate for failure of one instrument by cross referencing the others. It was a vital skill for any unit headed for cloudy European skies.[2]

On the surface, LeMay exuded can-do confidence. But beneath the stiff appearance (the right side of his face was paralyzed with Bell's Palsey, the result of a high-altitude flight), LeMay had the same doubts as any combat-bound commander. He asked himself how he would stand up to combat, wondering if he had the nerve to ask his men to do likewise.[3]

+===+===+

LeMay realized that if he were to lead successfully, he could not afford to let his men sense his doubts. His fliers called him The Old Man (he was thirty-five), as he possessed the knowledge and ability that would take them to Axis targets—and presumably home again. He maintained a positive, competent image for "the troops" while concealing his inner doubts. Like most of his contemporaries in the greatly expanded air force, he had received rapid promotion—three times in less than three years—and he perennially wondered if he were up to the task.

Then he got on with the war.

LeMay knew that he faced a huge task in getting the fledgling group operational, let alone combat capable. It was the difference between driving a race car around the block and being competitive on the track. There was so much to be done, and at first it had to be accomplished with scarce assets: too few airplanes, too few qualified pilots. Most of his pilots came straight from basic training with no experience in B-17s. Hardly any had ever flown a bomber in formation.

It was no better with aircrews. The 305th received some of its navigators just two weeks before deploying; many gunners arrived only days before. The latter were a perennial worry, as LeMay considered gunnery an essential skill. Drawing upon his early childhood, he believed that American males should know how to shoot, yet very few of his hastily trained gunners could hit more than the ground. And they would be facing the most experienced fighter pilots on earth.

In 1942 the Luftwaffe fighter arm, the Jagdwaffe, possessed potent aircraft such as the Messerschmitt 109 and Focke-Wulf 190, flown by seasoned professionals, many of whom were veterans of three years of combat. Many German aces had already claimed scores of kills against the British and Russians, and they did not fear the American newcomers.

In 1939 the Luftwaffe had driven Royal Air Force bombers from daytime skies, forcing the British to resort to night bombing. But the Americans, firm in their conviction that precision daylight attacks could help win the war, were determined to validate their doctrine. In that context, LeMay and the 305th faced an enormous challenge: prove the advantages of daylight bombardment deep in hostile airspace, without benefit of friendly fighter escort.

To England

The 305th's ground echelon sailed for Britain in September 1942, leaving four unsupported squadrons to continue last-minute training. After touring various western bases, and finally equipped with thirty-five new B-17Fs, the air echelon departed Syracuse, New

York. LeMay felt like the proverbial bandit getting out of Dodge City, one jump ahead of "the law," as he had been alerted that his airplanes and crews might be diverted to the Pacific, where General MacArthur needed more planes. Not wasting a moment, LeMay led his Fortresses eastward: Presque Isle, Maine; Gander, Newfoundland; and Prestwick, Scotland. He likened his mission to a children's crusade, considering how little training his crews had received—especially his navigators.

A few Fortresses were delayed with ground accidents or unmanageable propellers, but eventually the entire 305th Bombardment Group was reunited in Great Britain. LeMay heaved a sigh of relief—for the moment.

Upon arrival, LeMay encountered an old friend, Colonel Frank Armstrong, who possessed the invaluable advantage of some combat experience. LeMay corralled his colleague and pumped him for information. It all boiled down to one comment: Any bomber that flew straight and level for even ten seconds was bound be shot down. LeMay accepted the assessment as gospel and tucked it away.[4]

Then he set about establishing the 305th at its operational airfield, Grafton-Underwood in Northhamptonshire. The base was incomplete but the weather was persistent. LeMay overheard the control tower talking to one of his aircraft commanders, asking if the fliers could see the runway lights.

The pilot replied, "I can't even see my copilot!"[5]

The 305th was only the fourth bomb group of more than forty that joined the Eighth Air Force, tasked with bombing strategic targets in occupied Europe. The group's first mission, twentieth for "the Mighty Eighth," was logged November 17, a trip over German-occupied France. The 305th flew a diversionary route, not even armed with bombs, to draw enemy attention away from the thirty-five main force attackers at Saint-Nazaire. No bombers were lost but nearly half were damaged by flak and fighters.

Sometime later, LeMay heard from his younger brother Leonard, an engineering officer in North Africa, where Germans and Vichy French confronted the Allies. Curt never lived down the fact that his kid brother got shot at first.[6]

Meanwhile, LeMay set out to find photographs of likely targets in France. He found a good supply of reconnaissance imagery but almost nothing showing bomb damage assessment. Finally he discovered an awful truth: The U.S. Army Air Force did not know where at least half its bombs struck. Most targets were hardly scratched, despite the glowing PR reports released to the public. The bombing, concluded LeMay, was "stinko."[7]

Much later it was learned that in the early part of the war, the Royal Air Force (RAF) was only putting 20 percent of its bombs within five miles of the target. Therein lay the doctrinal difference between the British and Americans. The RAF, faced with appalling early losses in daylight, had switched to nocturnal bombing. Because of the limited technology available and poor night visibility, only cities were viable targets. Losses were still heavy (more than half of RAF Bomber Command aircrew were killed or captured), but at least the Brits were making an impact.

American airmen stuck to their guns—literally and figuratively—by insisting upon "precision" daylight bombardment. Partly it was doctrine, partly a high degree of confidence in the Norden bomb sight, but there was also "the old frontier pride in marksmanship."[8]

Hand in glove with daylight bombing was the belief in the self-defending bomber. After the war, LeMay conceded that almost nobody flying in Europe believed that unescorted bombers could operate safely, but there was no choice. America had no suitable long-range fighters so the only option was to send bombers alone. Lockheed P-38s could fly to Berlin but were plagued by high-altitude engine problems, and short-ranged Republic P-47s could only reach the German border. That summer, arrival of the fabled North American P-51 Mustang was a year and a half away.

After the first few missions, LeMay was convinced that the American bombing system needed overhaul. Typically, he began with himself, moving from the pilot's seat to the top turret. There he had an unobstructed view of the group formation and could critique each squadron's performance upon landing.

He also began questioning the conventional wisdom about evasive action. Pioneers like Frank Armstrong advocated a turning, "jinking" approach to the target with a ten-second straight run to the release point. LeMay knew better. Even with experienced bombardiers like John B. Montgomery (of the 1938 *Rex* intercept) and Doug Kilpatrick (of the 1937 USS *Utah* bombings), accuracy evaporated on such a short attack heading. There simply was not enough time to align the target in the sight for optimum accuracy.

Consequently, LeMay laid down the law: no evasive maneuvers from the initial reference point to "bombs away" when the ordnance was released. Contrary to contemporary doctrine, the 305th was going to fly straight and level, giving its bombardiers the best possible shot at the target. His crews wailed loud and long, but LeMay's logic was unassailable: Far better to take some losses while inflicting heavy damage on a target rather than have to return and try again another day.

Early experience showed that German fighter pilots preferred to attack damaged bombers and loose formations. Consequently, LeMay worked his squadrons hard, improving their formation flying skills and teaching the men to ignore their own stragglers. Soon he found the ideal layout: a "combat box" of eighteen to twenty-one bombers, staggered in altitude to bring as many guns to bear as possible.

In a combat box the lead squadron flew an assigned altitude with the low squadron flying below to one side while the high squadron formed above and to the opposite side. The result was a three-tiered formation that permitted each squadron to maneuver independently, if needed, while retaining group cohesion.

The B-17F had at least nine heavy machine guns: two each in top and bottom turrets, two at the waist, two in the tail, and one in the nose. When each Fortress was properly deployed in squadron and group formation, its defensive firepower was multiplied by the support it received from its wingmates. Thus, a dense pattern of machine gun fire greeted any attacking fighter.

Fighters could be intimidated by heavy firepower. But while there was no escaping flak, LeMay thought he had a partial solution. The old artilleryman dug into his ROTC manuals and consulted firing tables for the French 75mm weapon—not as effective as the German 88 but close enough for comparison. LeMay computed that it was necessary to fire nearly 400 rounds of high-explosive ammunition to hit a specific bomber at 25,000 feet.[9] Those were long odds but clearly they favored the target aircraft. The acid test came over St. Nazaire on November 23.

The mission was flown by portions of five groups, most of which launched barely half of the scheduled aircraft. Still, losses were heavy. The Ninety-first Group lost all five planes that reached the target; the 306th lost one of four.

The 305th put sixteen planes over France. All returned.

LeMay confided that the muzzle flashes of German fighters could be disconcerting, but his crews kept their wits and kept formation. Post-strike photos proved that the 305th put more bombs on target than the rest of the mission combined.[10]

Curt LeMay had made his case. Flying the box defensive formation, and making a straight-in run to the target without evasive maneuvers, produced exceptional results. Other units took notice.

Within weeks the 305th formula became known, then accepted. Eventually LeMay's box was standard for the Eighth Air Force, as it afforded mutual protection, massed firepower, and improved bombing accuracy. If LeMay had done nothing else in his career, he would be remembered for his innovative tactics in 1942–43. It may not be excessive to say that he saved daylight bombardment from oblivion.

In December the 305th moved to Chelveston, Northampton, west of Cambridge. The move interfered with combat missions—

only four were flown that month—but the group remained at "Station 105" for the rest of the war.

In the new year of 1943, LeMay turned his analytical powers to the tactical problems facing heavy bombers. He quickly identified two main issues: sloppy formation flying and poor air discipline. Both were anathema to precision bombing, as the larger the formation the wider the bomb pattern on the ground. Experimenting with various techniques, LeMay hit upon "bomb on lead." The group's head bombardier, being chosen as the most accurate, would release his load, signaling the others to drop their bombs at the same time.

With demonstrable results, the commanding officer (CO) was proud of his pilots and lauded them in a letter to Bob Olds, saying that he had stopped worrying whether a pilot with 350 hours could fly the airplane.[11]

On January 27, 1943, the Eighth attacked naval targets in northern Germany—the first time American heavy bombers penetrated Reich airspace. LeMay's old friend Frank Armstrong led the mission with the 306th group. Behind him were fifty-two other bombers. The primary target, Vegesack, was weathered in, so Armstrong took his "fleet" to the alternate, Wilhelmshaven, bombing through broken clouds. There was no opposition over the target but some sixty German fighters intercepted thereafter. A running gunfight developed, with three bombers lost. In turn, the Americans gleefully claimed twenty-two enemy planes destroyed.

LeMay did not believe it. He thought that most bomber gunners were firing long, undisciplined bursts and seldom hitting anything. He was proven right when, after the war, Luftwaffe records showed only seven fighters lost.

Back at Chelveston, LeMay was known as "Old Iron Ass" for ordering an immediate practice mission after the historic strike into Germany. He demanded tighter formations and straighter shooting, then took a risk that few commanders would even consider. He stood before his aircrews and declared, "If you think your group commander is a stupid son of a bitch, now is the time to say it. And why."[12]

Junior officers were astonished and noncoms were flabbergasted. Not only had the CO asked what they thought—he had invited criticism of himself. It was unheard of, but before long the 305th developed an institutional ethic. Everyone was entitled to a say, and if it made sense, Colonel LeMay likely would accept it and adopt a policy change. "The Old Man" believed that everyone should be equally involved. Amid flak and fighters the CO appeared unflappable: the crews with whom he flew said he appeared utterly calm, though the man himself admitted to vigorous butterflies and intestinal flip-flops. He always wanted his aircrews to see a commander who led from the front.

Some fliers still griped at post-mission practices and extra work at bombing, navigation, or gunnery, but nobody could argue with results. Curt LeMay was putting more bombs on target (though he was seldom satisfied) with fewer losses than other groups.

After only a couple of months on operations, LeMay was able to draw some conclusions. He checked the statistics and found a contradiction: The 305th was consistently putting up more planes than any other group, and its gunners were shooting more but they were hitting less. However, there was a symbiotic relationship among the figures.

Ben Fulkrod's maintenance crews spared no effort to keep the most possible bombers airworthy. Where some groups averaged perhaps a dozen, Chelveston nearly always launched twenty-plus. That translated into more guns in the air, producing a denser pattern of fire. Beyond that, with LeMay's blessing, Major Ralph Cohen's armament section advocated opening fire at maximum range. Consequently, Luftwaffe fighters took note and sought easier prey. Other groups claimed more shootdowns, but the 305th was subjected to fewer aggressive attacks, with fewer bombers lost.

That summer LeMay recognized a pattern in some poorly executed missions. The crews leading some missions had never seen the target before, resulting in misidentification or late recognition, leading to insufficient time for a proper bomb run.

LeMay's solution was the "lead crew" concept: selecting specific pilots, navigators, and bombardiers to become the group's authorities on specific targets. Before a mission they were closeted in a special room with photos and maps of the target area, studying the material from every possible approach, even in varying light conditions. Eventually lead crews became so proficient that they could recognize "their" target even through low clouds. Consequently, bombing accuracy and mission efficiency improved so quickly that General Eaker's Eighth Bomber Command adopted the policy for all groups in July 1943.

On April 4, 1943, the 305th attacked a Renault truck factory in Paris with impressive results. Bombing from 22,000 feet, LeMay's squadrons (this time led by Major Thomas K. McGehee) put almost eighty tons of ordnance on target, reducing Renault production for six months. The Luftwaffe arrived late but stayed to party: Perhaps seventy Focke-Wulf 190s attacked for nearly an hour after "bombs away," making company-front attacks at the Forts. The 364th squadron lost three of the four planes downed on the mission but the group kept its formation, as LeMay had taught.

Subsequently the 305th received a Distinguished Unit Citation for the mission: proof that LeMay's "children's crusade" was growing up.

There were other losses that spring, neither in combat but both bitterly painful. Bob Olds died of a rare heart disease in April and Frank Andrews perished in a B-24 accident the next month. LeMay suffered the loss of two irreplaceable friends and mentors more keenly than he showed, but their personal influence upon him continued to yield institutional benefits. Perhaps without realizing it, LeMay was following in their philosophical contrails.

In 1943 the Eighth Air Force was the only major U.S. command engaging Germany in northern Europe, and consequently it was the focus of much press coverage. Among the correspondents who visited Chelveston was novelist MacKinlay Kantor, who had flown on some missions with the RAF. LeMay granted his request to see Occupied Europe from a B-17, leading to a lasting friendship. In 1945 Kantor wrote a blank verse novel called *Glory for Me,* based in large part on his experiences with the 305th. It became the basis for the acclaimed postwar screenplay *The Best Years of Our Lives.*

LeMay retained command until May, when he was scheduled to be relieved by Lieutenant Colonel Donald K. Fargo. If LeMay was sentimental about any portion of his long career, it was probably the eleven months he spent leading the 305th.

LeMay served a brief stint leading the temporary Provisional Combat Wing before taking the Fourth Wing, which was soon expanded into the Third Air Division in September 1943. LeMay moved to his new command on the Suffolk coast, "a weird and wonderful place" called Elveden.[13]

When LeMay took over the Third Division (composed of four wings, each with two or more groups), he found himself building a new force. As of April only two bomb groups had entered combat, the Ninety-fourth and Ninety-fifth, with the Ninety-sixth going operational in May. However, by year's end his four combat wings numbered eight groups with more en route.

Despite his exceptional success, LeMay did not take his rapid rise for granted. He had felt barely capable of running a squadron when he assumed command of a group, and there was still much to learn in that role when he got the division. Considering the situation in retrospect, he said it was like straddling a barbed wire fence.

By now LeMay was overtaking some of his prewar commanders. Upon taking the Third Division he found Colonel Alfred A. Kessler leading the new Ninety-fifth Group. Kessler, who had been LeMay's second squadron commander, said, "Don't worry about it, Curt.

You've been in combat; I haven't. . . . Let's forget that I was ever your squadron commander."[14]

As a group and wing commander, LeMay had to deal with human factors as well as materiel: men wore out faster than airplanes. In spite of his "Iron Ass" reputation, he demonstrated a combination of compassion leavened with what a later generation would call "tough love."

In 1943, Eighth Air Force bomber losses were running at 4 percent or more: sometimes twice that figure. Fliers computed the odds of surviving a twenty-five-mission tour as exactly zero, but aircrew continued to fly with a sense of fatalism. However, LeMay noted that when losses dropped, combat fatigue increased. He concluded that, with little prospect of survival, mental breakdowns were almost nonexistent because fliers accepted their fate.[15]

Faced with pilots and crewmen who had reached their limit, LeMay often found ways to return them to duty. Where other commanders berated men as slackers or cowards, "Colonel Iron Ass" transferred them to nonflying duty for awhile. One bomber pilot returned with dead crewmen on three consecutive missions and refused to chauffeur other men to their doom. Offered a transfer to a single-seat fighter, the B-17 man leapt at the chance and, given a P-47, shot down four Germans.

LeMay also left his stamp on men with whom he had nothing in common philosophically. After the war, one of his navigators became a liberal activist, a civil liberties lawyer who rose to prominence as an activist judge. When the jurist's colleagues learned that he had named his son for LeMay, they were astonished. But the judge explained that he owed his life—and therefore his son's existence—to Curtis Emerson LeMay.[16]

Despite his seniority, LeMay continued flying combat, including some of "the rough ones," such as the double-strike mission of August 17, 1943: dual attacks against Regensburg and Schweinfurt. It was a bold, innovative plan: two aerial task forces striking enemy production centers simultaneously, with the Regensburg bombers proceeding south to Africa.

On that day, LeMay led seven groups (146 B-17s) to hit the Messerschmitt factory at Regensburg, sixty miles southeast of Nuremburg. The Schweinfurt force of 230 First Division Fortresses remained grounded by heavy fog at first, but since LeMay had drilled his Third Division crews incessantly, they made instrument takeoffs, all successfully.

Flying with the Ninety-sixth group, LeMay learned that the First Division had not taken off as scheduled. It was time for a command decision: Without the Schweinfurt attack to split the defenses, his relatively small armada would face the bulk of Germany's fighter force. Lieutenant General Ira Eaker, chief of "the Mighty Eighth," gave the word: proceed to Regensburg. Messerschmitts and Focke-Wulfs began interceptions over Belgium; the P-47 fighter escorts were too few and poorly positioned to lend much help.

The Germans were "right good" in LeMay's estimation. He quipped, "Our fighter escort had black crosses on their wings." When his force turned onto its bomb run at Nuremburg it retained 131 of the original 146 bombers. LeMay's wing had escaped the worst of it, losing two Forts among sixty-two dispatched.[17]

Over Regensburg, the Americans had things their own way. LeMay marveled at the sudden absence of interceptors, and the flak was sporadic. Clearly visible, the large factory complex lay wide open to attack. Employing LeMay's "drop on lead" technique, his bombers unloaded when Lieutenant Dunstan Abel of the Ninety-sixth called "bombs away."[18]

Hangars and workshops were pounded by some 300 tons of high explosive and incendiary bombs. The attack lasted twenty-two minutes, striking nearly every building in the complex. The target was reckoned at 50 percent destroyed.

Coming off the target, LeMay's force attracted twin-engine fighters that knocked down more Fortresses. Nevertheless, the task force headed south, churning toward Africa at 160 mph. The Alps passed beneath the Boeings, then the expanse of the Mediterranean.

The Regensburg survivors descended toward two Algerian fields. LeMay alit from his aircraft after eleven hours and surveyed his sandy domain. Major General Lauris Norstad, operations officer for Northwest Africa, had told him to expect a well-equipped air depot to service and repair his bombers, but the war had passed Tunisia and rolled eastward. LeMay's destination, Telergma, had become a backwater.

Then the debriefing began. At first Colonel Beirne Lay of Eaker's staff approached LeMay. Lay had ridden with the One-hundredth group, which sustained heavy losses. He told the force commander that other trailing groups also were hard hit. LeMay was taken aback: flying near the head of the fifteen-mile procession, the Ninety-sixth lost no aircraft. But eventually the numbers were compiled and it became obvious that twenty-four Regensburg attackers had been destroyed. It was an appalling figure: one in six.

The Schweinfurt force lost thirty-six planes; 15 percent, plus others that would never fly again. Over sixty bombers were destroyed or written off: a stunning figure. The previous one-mission record loss was twenty-six.

Despite the casualties, and the unknown but large number of unflyable planes that would be delayed in Africa, the aggressive LeMay wanted to hit more targets on the return trip. Eaker approved, reckoning that an attack both outbound and inbound would have an effect on friends and enemies alike.

+≈≈≈+

As wing commander, LeMay continued his crews' on-the-job education. There was constant reason to worry: always the weather; usually the bombing results; frequently replacement crews and aircraft. The first two became the loci of another concern—radar.

In 1943–44 radar appeared to be the answer to the Eighth Air Force's dilemma. Trained in precision daylight bombing, the crews were frustrated time and again by heavy undercast that obscured their targets. The electronic eye of radar posed a likely solution, but it had yet to live up to its promise. Radar worked best on coastal targets, since shorelines easily stood out, but farther inland the radar picture was often obscured by mixed signal returns or "ground clutter." LeMay decided to study the new technology and apply his analytical skills to making it work better.

In November 1943, shortly after the second Schweinfurt mission, LeMay was sent home for a publicity tour with other Eighth Air Force leaders. A reunion with Helen and not-quite-five Janie was all too brief before he hit the lecture circuit.

During World War II, all the armed forces were institutionally aware of the benefit of public relations for recruiting and funding. But individual officers were seldom as media savvy as those today, and few were less interested in the subject than newly promoted Brigadier General LeMay, who was assigned a speech writer.

LeMay's speeches were produced by a staff officer, Sidney "Sy" Bartlett, who had fifteen movies to his credit, and later coauthored *Twelve O'Clock High*. Though generally reluctant to speak in public, one of LeMay's pet peeves was the typical description of bomber operations as "raids." Taking advantage of the opportunity to explain the situation, he described bomber missions as "full-scale battles, fought in the thin air, miles above the land."[19]

Returning to Elveden a month later, LeMay found things little changed. He was still concerned with gunnery and, having harped on the subject during visits to training command bases, he resumed his campaign to improve the volume and accuracy of bomber defensive fire.

⊬══⊬

The new year brought accelerating change. In January 1944, Lieutenant General Jimmy Doolittle became commander of the Eighth Air Force, with Ira Eaker rotating to the Mediterranean. Lieutenant

General Carl Spaatz assumed the position of commander, Strategic Air Forces in Europe, and a major campaign was launched in late February. It was called "Big Week."

Aimed at the German aircraft industry, Big Week fought the climate as much as the Luftwaffe. On February 22, 1944, third day of the blitz, bad weather forced an abort. LeMay issued a recall order to his Third Division, though in the confusion of combat some airborne commanders were uncertain of its validity. With recall of the Second Division, only the First bombed worthwhile targets.

It was one of the few occasions in which the rest of the Eighth Air Force inflicted more damage than LeMay's command.

In March 1944, when he pinned on his second star, LeMay became, at thirty-seven, the youngest major general not only in the AAF, but in the U.S. Army. Shortly he received new orders, sending him home to supervise the Boeing B-29 program. There was no greater responsibility in the air force, as the Superfortress became the costliest program of the war: three billion dollars.

LeMay could not resist a look at the ground war before leaving Europe. Shortly after D-Day he called Major General William Kepner, commander of the Eighth's fighters, asking to borrow a P-47 and "have a look around." Kepner, thirteen years LeMay's senior, replied, "I'll go with you, Curt."[20]

The two generals landed at an advanced airfield in France and encountered Brigadier General James W. McCauley, commanding a Ninth Air Force wing. The trio—with five stars among them—took a command car toward the front lines.

Kepner insisted on looking beyond each rise, and soon the fliers were well forward; they saw dead Germans and heard shellfire. LeMay knew something of Kepner's exceptional background—he had been a marine before World War I and led an army battalion in 1918—but the flying generals were unescorted and unarmed. However, such concerns were forgotten when they found a mint-condition Opel sedan with a dead battery. They towed the prize away behind McCauley's command car, ducking artillery explosions en route.

When he left England, LeMay had accomplished as much as anyone could in his position. He had trained a rag-tag bomb group with minimal assets, taken it to combat, and forged it into a competent weapon. Furthermore, he was largely responsible for two important tactical innovations: the box defensive formation and the straight-and-level, nonevasive bombing run. Both became standard operating procedure in the European Theater. Beyond that, he had led the Regensburg mission as a division commander, willingly exposing himself to additional combat hazard. If he had done nothing else, Curt LeMay's reputation was assured.

CHAPTER 4

China

Upon returning to the United States, Major General LeMay's first priority was flying the B-29 Superfortress. He felt that he could not effectively command an air force without a firm grasp of its primary aircraft, regardless of how much he might fly it in-theater. Consequently, he qualified as a command pilot in the B-29 at Boeing's Wichita plant.

The '29 had been conceived in 1940 when America feared that Germany might conquer Britain, depriving U.S. bombers of allied bases. Therefore, the Superfortress was designed for flying very long-range missions. LeMay, however, found the project had "as many 'bugs' as the Smithsonian Institution's entomological department."[1]

It had been said of the B-17 that it only had four problems: its 1,200-horsepower Wright R1820 Cyclone engines, known for leaking oil. In marked contrast, the B-29's huge eighteen-cylinder

R3350 "Duplex Cyclones" were rated at 2,200 horsepower—almost twice the B-17 engines—but caused far more than twice the problems.

The R3350 engine produced a daunting variety of woes for B-29 crews. Configured as a twin-bank radial, the rear row of cylinders did not receive sufficient cooling, which prompted a variety of ills. The duplex engines showed a distressing tendency to swallow valves in flight, causing internal fires. Frequently the magnesium cases then burned in a manner the crew could not contain.

Nor was that all. The convex plexiglass blisters in the fuselage gunners' stations either iced over, obscuring visibility, or blew out from pressurization problems. Boeing and the military devoted enormous effort to curing those and other concerns, but it was an ongoing process requiring endless hard work.

LeMay was neither surprised nor overly distressed at the B-29's continuing troubles. Having matured with the B-17, he knew that years of prewar experience had eliminated nearly all the bugs from the Fortress's airframe and engines before the first bomber landed in England. In contrast, the Superfortress, built almost entirely after Pearl Harbor, had the benefit of only a fraction of the peacetime development of its elegant predecessor.

Despite its complexity, LeMay quickly took the measure of the new Boeing. When told that bombing accuracy was hampered by frost accumulating on the bombardier's nose panels, he responded almost casually, advising that the glass should be completely cleaned before the mission, while the aircraft interior could be dried by opening all windows before climbing to cruise altitude. Should frost still form, LeMay told his crews to depressurize the aircraft and open the windows. He knew from prewar experience that they could fly at 40 degrees below zero with the windows open yet remain reasonably warm inside.[2]

LeMay had complete technical mastery of his profession. He was by no means the only general in the Army Air Forces to possess such knowledge, but he was the only one who could bring the service's most expensive and most capable weapon system to near technical and operational perfection. Throughout his career, from second lieutenant to chief of staff, the bedrock of his leadership was professional competence. His subordinates learned that Curt LeMay probably knew at least as much about their work as they did, prompting them to scramble to keep ahead of "The Old Man."

While LeMay was mastering the Superfortress, China-based B-29s had begun operations in June, flying two missions totaling 145 sorties (takeoffs by individual aircraft). Two more missions in July yielded just 85 sorties.

LeMay took a Douglas C-54 to Kharagpur, India, arriving August 29. He found a near chaotic situation characterized by constant shortages. There was almost no fuel for training missions, and no firm doctrine for operating the new bombers. Though most of the aircraft commanders were experienced pilots, they had little idea how to best employ their new Boeings as weapons, and none had ever flown in the mountainous terrain between India and China.

Part of the problem was a lack of continuity of leadership. The India-China operation had first been handed to Brigadier General Kenneth B. Wolfe, an engineering officer who had helped bring the B-29 into service. But he was shortly replaced by one of LeMay's flying school classmates: Brigadier General Laverne G. Saunders.

"Blondie" Saunders was well known in the service, being a former West Point football coach. He had been in Hawaii on December 7, 1941, and later flew bomber missions in the Solomon Islands. In July 1943 Saunders formed the Fifth-eighth Bomb Wing, the first equipped with B-29s. He took his squadrons to India in April 1944, and was named to lead XX Bomber Command in early July, pending LeMay's arrival. In mid-September Saunders flew to an outlying field to say farewell to friends, then took off in a North American B-25 Mitchell and disappeared en route back to Kharagpur.

When Saunders failed to return, LeMay ordered an immediate search along the flight path, but that night the new commander had second thoughts. He knew Saunders as a meticulous professional; the fact that Blondie had not reported setting his course led LeMay to conclude that the Mitchell had crashed shortly after takeoff. LeMay and Colonel Alfred F. Kalberer flew to the field and almost immediately spotted a gouge in the jungle near the runway. They landed, followed a compass bearing, and found Saunders critically injured with one other survivor. A crane truck lifted a Wright engine off Saunders's leg, which eventually was amputated. He was medically retired in 1947 but remained close to LeMay, who likely had saved his life by conducting a personal search.

The rescue operation was typical of LeMay: Though far senior to the other pilots seeking the missing aircraft, he seized the initiative and used his professional reasoning to solve the problem. It may have been the only time that a major general personally went looking for a missing brigadier, but the difference in their ranks probably never occurred to LeMay. Blondie Saunders was a valued friend of some fifteen years, and Curt LeMay had the means and the knowledge to help find him. That brand of up-front leadership was a LeMay trademark, for whatever his faults, they did not include fickleness.

In Saunders's absence, LeMay could rely upon other staffers for support. Among the most valuable was Colonel Kalberer, a prewar airline pilot in the United States and Holland. Having flown multiengine aircraft all over the world, Kalberer possessed exceptional knowledge of weather and operating conditions in Europe and Asia. Kalberer arose to command of the 462nd Bomb Group in August 1944, the month that LeMay arrived in India. He had already distinguished himself in the Mediterranean Theater, and quickly gained LeMay's confidence.

All manner of problems emerged in India, big and small. They ranged from inadequate fuel supplies—seven ferry flights across the Himalayas were necessary for one combat sortie—to inadequate maps. LeMay learned from one of his group commanders that available maps were almost useless: Some had no height information and others were just plain wrong. LeMay, the old airmail pilot, applied the conventional wisdom to the situation: "Add a couple of thousand feet for yourself and three thousand more for the wife and kids."

Though he seldom said so at the time, LeMay had serious doubts about the viability of sustaining B-29 operations in China. As an enormously complex weapon system (some 55,000 parts) the Superfortress placed unprecedented demands upon maintenance and logistics. Operating the world's most sophisticated aircraft at the end of the world's longest supply line made little sense to the pragmatic young general. But as he often stated, once an officer's objections had been noted, he was obliged to carry out superiors' orders. Nevertheless, when offered additional B-29 groups by commander of the Army Air Forces General Henry H. Arnold, LeMay declined them. He was already conducting ferry flights across "the Hump," the high mountains from India into China, bringing enough fuel to mount small-scale missions one at a time. More bombers would only complicate matters, so he made do with the four groups on hand.

The Twentieth Air Force was unlike any other fielded during World War II. Though Saunders, Haywood Hansell, and LeMay led in the field, Hap Arnold retained overall command from Washington. He felt that four- (and later, five-) star leadership was necessary to prevent the B-29s from being tasked to non-strategic missions by army or navy theater commanders. However, Arnold's health declined in 1944 and he was frequently unable to devote as much attention to the Twentieth as he may have liked.

The command's primary facilities were eight fields spread around Kharagpur, India, including four supporting the C-109 tankers providing fuel to Chinese operating bases. But the bases lay 1,300 miles northeast of Kharagpur, in the Chengtu area of Szechuan Province. No other air arm operated over such a vast expanse with so rudimentary facilities. The Chengtu runways had literally been built by hand, thanks largely to the incessant toiling of thousands of Chinese workers, called coolies.

Much as LeMay had done in England, he began revising procedures and tactics in Asia. He stopped most of the four-plane night missions in preference for twelve-plane daylight formations, employing the combat box formation he had developed in Europe. He also set about identifying lead crews and began streamlining the maintenance program.

Ever the technician, LeMay reviewed his crews' performance and immediately saw ways to improve efficiency. He stressed "cruise control," milking the most from each gallon of fuel, both because it afforded more range and had the potential to increase bomb loads. Hand in glove with his lead crew policy, he began a shift from individual bombing to "drop on lead," when the designated bombardier toggled his bombs. Gradually, bomb patterns on targets began tightening up.

Before long, LeMay was agitating to fly some missions himself. His superiors were aghast—major generals knew far too much to risk capture by the Japanese—but LeMay was adamant. Finally granted permission for one flight, he consulted the target list and settled on Anshan, Manchuria. It provided steel to Japanese industry, and was sure to be well defended. That suited LeMay, who wanted a look at enemy fighter tactics. Anshan reputedly hosted a nest of aggressive interceptors.

The logistics effort to mount the Anshan mission was enormous. Nearly one thousand tanker flights had been necessary to accumulate sufficient fuel stocks to top off the bombers.

Leading 101 B-29s—a major effort at the time—LeMay took his bombers to Chengtu, China, and launched against Anshan on September 8. Enemy fighters were up but poorly positioned; only one got close enough to shoot, but the flak remained a problem.

LeMay's plane took a hit, and two crewmen cried that they were wounded. LeMay grabbed a first aid kit and first checked the radio operator. The youngster sheepishly discovered that his flak vest had stopped just a large splinter. Next LeMay looked at the primary gunner. That airman had merely received a scraped knuckle; LeMay glowered at both and returned to the flight deck.

Based on what he saw during the mission, LeMay's original opinion of XX Bomber Command was only reinforced. He took an unprecedented action: He stood down the entire command for an intense period of retraining. He was in charge and his air force was going to learn to do things his way.

In truth, the Superfortresses were not grounded—they merely stood down from operations. Basically, LeMay applied the same remedies he had employed with the 305th Group in England: standardizing procedures; identifying and training lead crews; tweaking every possible angle for increased efficiency. It was vintage LeMay, in part a legacy of the bitter lesson of Pearl Harbor when the Army Air Force—like the rest of America's military—was caught unprepared for war. Throughout his career, LeMay stressed training and preparedness, the twin pillars of his leadership philosophy. But nowhere was he more challenged than in the far-flung reaches of Asia.

Despite the obligation that Hap Arnold felt to deliver on the B-29's promise (it was the most expensive weapon system of the war), he remained supportive of LeMay from far-off Washington. Recognizing the wisdom of retraining XX Bomber Command in-theater, the Army Air Forces chief approved LeMay's unconventional practices while continuing to press for greater bomb loads.

LeMay already knew everything he needed to know about the relatively light bomb loads his planes were carrying. Remedying the situation was not as simple. Depending on distance to the target, the B-29s operated at or near maximum weight, which called several factors into play. Maximum permissible takeoff weight was determined by runway length and "density altitude," the equivalent elevation of an airfield in certain atmospheric conditions. The Chengtu fields lay at 1,700 feet above sea level, but on an eighty-degree day, depending on barometric pressure and dew point, the density altitude easily could exceed 3,500 feet. That required longer runways or lighter loads. Consequently, LeMay set about juggling the variables, setting fuel and bomb loads to comply with existing bases while urging runway extensions.

By mid-October XX Bomber Command had dialed in the numbers. On a mission flown the fourteenth, 104 of the 130 Superfortresses dispatched against aircraft factories at Okayama, Japan, each released 13,600 pounds of ordnance—three times the previous average. Arnold was so pleased that he began posting strike photos in Twentieth Air Force headquarters in D.C., proof that the big Boeing was starting to pay for itself.

Among those interested in XX Bomber Command's performance was a non-rated (wingless) officer from the Office of Statistical Control at Harvard. Lieutenant Colonel Robert S. McNamara had first seen B-29s when the Fifty-eighth Wing was forming in Kansas, and went to India to track their combat performance.

LeMay impressed the statistician as a particularly hard case: reportedly LeMay had recommended courts-martial for pilots who aborted missions because he was focused on one thing: target destruction. He even kept his own statistics including loss of crews per target destroyed. While critics might contend that it demonstrated a cold-bloodedness in LeMay, in truth it was simply a method of assessing his command's military efficiency.

Whatever his personal opinions of LeMay, McNamara was forced to admit that the young general knew his business. Almost without exception, no heavy bomber command in the deployed Army Air Forces ever exceeded eighty hours per aircraft per month. Yet from China, LeMay was getting over ninety hours per airframe, and not with tried-and-true B-17s or B-24s, but with the world's most sophisticated bomber—one that had not yet reached maturity.[3]

Even more remarkably, McNamara's figures showed that XX Bomber Command nearly matched stateside B-29 operations, which were supported by a much larger maintenance operation.

Despite much improved maintenance, among LeMay's other problems was a natural phenomenon almost wholly unknown before the war: the jet stream. Though discovered in the 1920s, the very fast winds above 25,000 to 30,000 feet came as a surprise in World War II because few aircraft had routinely flown that high. In winter the stream averaged about seventy-five mph, scattering bombs in erratic patterns far from their targets. LeMay and his tacticians tackled the challenge, but it resisted their best efforts.

There were of course nontechnical, nonoperational problems. The geopolitical situation in China was enormously complex. There were essentially three governments: Chiang Kai-shek's nationalists in the south; Mao Tse-tung's communists in the north; and the Japanese. The latter controlled most of the coast and the desirable ports, but retained ambitions well inland. In the summer and fall of 1944 the Japanese launched a massive offensive that overran many of Major General Claire Chennault's Fourteenth Air Force bases, and threatened the B-29 fields in the Chengtu Valley. Though LeMay's fields were safe, the China-Burma-India command recognized that it was due more to poor weather and Japanese supply problems than anything else.

Military politics also proved difficult for LeMay, whose command was pulled in different (sometimes contradictory) directions by various leaders. The overall allied commander in the China-Burma-India (CBI) Theater was a British admiral, the charming, capable Lord Louis Mountbatten. When LeMay arrived, the senior American in the CBI was a blunt, irascible infantryman: General Joseph W. Stilwell, who loudly proclaimed his skepticism of airpower. While LeMay reported to neither Mountbatten nor Stilwell—Arnold commanded Twentieth Air Force in Washington—LeMay was still obliged to get along with the top allied leaders who had a claim on his resources. As it was, he only saw Mountbatten once, and Stilwell was soon replaced by General Albert C. Wedemeyer.

With improved logistics, the B-29 sortie count had slowly improved before LeMay arrived, reaching 131 in August. Thereafter, his methods began taking effect: The huge Boeings flew more and more: 200-plus sorties both in September and October, with 316 in five missions during November and 330 during five December missions.

Despite LeMay's encouraging record, deteriorating weather began interfering with B-29 operations. Heavy clouds over Japan and much of the Asian mainland forced bombardiers to rely upon radar during the winter months, with an attendant loss of accuracy. On one of XX Bomber Command's three largest missions, November 21, only 61 of 109 planes bombed the primary target at Omura while 17 others hit alternates. The balance—nearly 30 percent of the force—were unable to identify any targets on Kyushu or along the China coast. Furthermore, six planes were lost.

Another constant difficulty was the perennial fuel shortage. LeMay, ever tracking the consumption, computed that even with C-109 tankers available, over one-third of B-29 flight hours were devoted to tanker or cargo operations. It further validated his initial impression that Superfortress operations in Asia were unsustainable. However, he continued operations as much as fuel supplies allowed.

Based on his European experience, LeMay of all people knew that combat operations resulted in casualties. While the destruction of a single B-29 represented a significant materiel and financial loss, LeMay was more concerned with retrieving as many of his aircrew as possible. He therefore established contact with Mao Tse-tung, dealing directly with the legendary communist leader, and eventually exchanged letters and gifts; LeMay received a captured Japanese sword in return for a fine pair of binoculars. But more importantly, XX Bomber Command was able to dispatch Douglas C-47s loaded with medical supplies and liaison officers to communist-controlled areas, and in return, Mao's forces prepared advanced landing fields for B-29s suffering battle damage or fuel shortage. In that respect, the Chinese Communists were far more cooperative than the Soviets, who provided very little weather data and held B-29s and their crews for months on end.

Chennault had convinced General Albert C. Wedemeyer, the new American theater commander, that an incendiary raid on the supply center of Hankow, China, would seriously disrupt Japanese operations in the area, and Wedemeyer asked XX Bomber Command to oblige. LeMay was indifferent to the prospects—he much preferred to strike Japanese homeland targets—and doubted Wedemeyer's authority over the Twentieth Air Force. But the joint chiefs often approved such "requests" from theater commanders, so on December 18 LeMay sent 84 Superfortresses to Hankow while Chennault contributed 200 more planes. The results were spectacular: The target area burned for three days and the 14th Air Force concluded that the city was "destroyed as a major base." Hankow had proven one of the few instances that LeMay's professional judgment had been in error.[4]

The devastating effect of incendiary bombs confirmed what Army Air Force analysts already suspected before the war: Once started, a conflagration could not be contained in most Asian cities, which were largely constructed of wood. LeMay and his targeting staff took note of the results and filed it for future reference.

By then the decision had already been made to transfer the B-29s to the Central Pacific, where logistics were far more manageable. Without delivering supplies via "the back door" in India, direct American access to Marianas bases ensured B-29 wings an uninterrupted flow of aircraft, crews, fuel, and bombs.

In January LeMay made a quick visit to Guam to assess the buildup of XXI Bomber Command in the Mariana Islands. He consulted with Hap Arnold's chief of staff, now Lieutenant General Lauris "Larry" Norstad, and learned of plans to phase out the China operation, moving all B-29s to the Pacific as fast as bases were completed. Largely satisfied with what he saw—the logistics situation was far better than in the CBI Theater—LeMay returned to China to relinquish XX Bomber Command to Brigadier General Roger

Ramey, formerly commander of V Bomber Command in the Southwest Pacific. By then the China-based Boeings were nearly out of worthwhile targets.

During the five months he led XX Bomber Command, LeMay considered results over Japan disappointing at best, largely owing to poor weather and the unexpected challenge of the jet stream. But the B-29s had proven their range and payload, striking targets at Formosa and as far south as Rangoon and Singapore. Thus, LeMay had built upon his predecessors' efforts and significantly improved the B-29 as a weapon system.

When he flew from China to the Marianas, LeMay was confident of what he could accomplish with much improved logistical support in the Pacific. Properly supplied, he would become the worst enemy of Imperial Japan.

CHAPTER 5

Marianas

IN THE CHINA-BURMA-INDIA THEATER, LEMAY HAD FOUGHT a three-front war against a long logistical pipeline, the complex Allied command structure, and the Japanese, in approximately that order. Having turned over XX Bomber Command in January 1945, he looked forward to a simpler mission in the Central Pacific, concentrating primarily upon the enemy rather than constant supply problems. Additionally, he would only have to coordinate with the U.S. Navy without concern for Chinese and British sensibilities.

LeMay arrived in the Marianas on January 20, 1945. Once there, he faced a tough situation: replacing Brigadier General Haywood S. Hansell, Jr., a longtime friend and associate.

"Possum" Hansell had coauthored the Air War Plan Division's AWPD-1, the Army's 1941 blueprint for conducting a modern air war. The planning committee's work was visionary, proving accurate

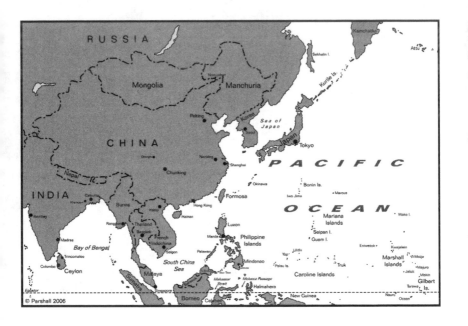

© Parshall 2006

within a few percentage points of the numbers of personnel and combat groups required. (The airmen erred in the capacity of American industry, which delivered 80,000 combat aircraft versus the 63,400 estimated.) Previously an Eighth Air Force wing commander, in October 1944 Hansell had arrived in the Marianas as leader of XXI Bomber Command. Hansell's B-29s had achieved no significant success, but LeMay nevertheless asked his former classmate to remain awhile, helping ease the transition.

Upon relieving Hansell, LeMay found several familiar faces. The operations officer was a Langley Field alumnus, now-Colonel John B. Montgomery who had flown with Olds's Second Bomb Group in the pioneering B-17 days. LeMay was pleased with the staff: He recognized many of the officers and knew that he could speak plainly to them, and they to him. It was the only way he ever functioned.

However, the new commander was already under pressure from Washington. Another young two-star, Lauris Norstad, who was General Hap Arnold's chief of staff for Twentieth Air Force operations, had day-to-day control of the B-29 force from Washington. With LeMay-like bluntness, Norstad wrote his colleague, "If you don't get results, you will be fired. There will never be any Strategic Air Forces of the Pacific after the battle is fully won in Europe and those European forces can be deployed to the Pacific. If you don't get results, it will mean eventually a mass amphibious invasion of Japan, to cost probably a half a million more American lives."[1]

Norstad, of course, had been the officer who assured LeMay that adequate fields awaited the Regensburg attackers in North Africa nearly a year and a half previously. However, the relationship between the two air commanders—an erstwhile artilleryman and a former cavalryman—remained mutually respectful if not warm; they had known one another since Hawaii a decade before. To Norstad, LeMay was "an operator; the rest of us are planners." To LeMay, Norstad was "one of those brilliant guys."[2] The two were not friends but they did not need to be: Each had his own responsibilities and in turn recognized the other's strengths.

LeMay inherited an operating command that was not producing results; it needed innovative leadership. The first XXI Bomber Command missions had been flown against the Caroline Islands in November. They were low-risk affairs, providing "warm-ups" for Brigadier General Emmett O'Donnell's pioneering Seventy-third Bomb Wing. O'Donnell's rise had been almost as rapid as LeMay's. A West Pointer, on December 7 "Rosey" had been a major in the Philippines; barely two years later he was a general.

On November 24, 1944, before LeMay's arrival, O'Donnell led more than 100 Tokyo-bound Superfortresses through miserable weather and hellacious winds aloft: Some bombardiers computed a groundspeed of 445 mph. Few bombers reached the target—some topped out at 35,000 feet—and damage inflicted was negligible.

On the following mission three days later, an incredible downwind groundspeed reached 580 mph. Bombing accuracy vanished. But Hansell decided there was no option except to continue according to doctrine, despite a suggestion from Norstad that incendiaries delivered from lower altitude could produce results.

When LeMay assumed command in January 1945, the Marianas B-29s had flown seventeen missions in eleven weeks, including eleven against Japan. Some 950 sorties had been launched, of which 780 had bombed anything, and far fewer had attacked primary targets. Thus, aborts and weather had consistently conspired to rob Hansell of one-fifth of his potential striking power. Losses had been steady and somewhat high: around 4.5 percent.

Most importantly, no targets had been destroyed.

LeMay found a curious anomaly regarding B-29 combat losses between XX and XXI Bomber Commands. In China the Superforts sustained far heavier casualties from Japanese fighters than flak (twenty-two to seven) while the Marianas losses were almost evenly divided (fifty-two to fighters; forty-seven to flak, with nineteen attributed to both). Having seen the effects of Luftwaffe on his B-17s, LeMay was concerned about the Japanese fighter threat to his force.[3]

In March, before the Marines had fully secured Iwo Jima, long-range fighters began arriving in the Bonin Islands, 750 miles south of Tokyo. Commander of VII Fighter Command was Brigadier General Earnest M. "Mickey" Moore, whose initial two P-51 groups flew their first long-range escort on April 7 and began taking a toll of enemy interceptors. B-29 losses to Japanese aircraft had peaked with a dozen each in January and April but thereafter dropped dramatically to none in July.

Meanwhile, LeMay's staff had scrutinized the logistics situation. With too few men and too little equipment to move the immense volume of ordnance from ships to bomb storage dumps to the waiting aircraft, LeMay decided to bypass the middle. He ordered incendiaries taken directly from dockside to the waiting B-29s. LeMay praised not only the navy, which finally could deliver enough bombs, but everyone ashore who could lend a hand. He found off-duty Navy Seabees and administrative personnel and even some marines who willingly set to work, often reckoning that the more bombs were moved, the sooner everyone could go home.

To his staff, LeMay conceded that weather was the main tactical problem—far more than the Japanese. But for the moment he decided to continue the doctrinal methods of strategic bombardment: high-level, daylight "precision" attacks.[4]

Despite the operational setbacks, there were improvements. By January 1945 Boeing's Seattle and Wichita plants had achieved large-scale production, averaging about 100 aircraft a month. That figure would triple in the last eight months of the war—an exceptional achievement in its own right, apart from the Superfort's technical success. But troubles remained, most notably cooling problems in the Wright R3350 Cyclone engines.

Logistics were far better in the Marianas than in China. The first ship to dock at Tinian Island was the transport *General Robert Olds*, named for LeMay's prewar mentor. With sealift assured, XXI

Bomber Command could rely upon a steady flow of fuel and bombs, while critically needed items such as spare parts could be flown in.

Among the invaluable members of LeMay's staff was Colonel C. S. Irvine, the A-4 (supply) officer. LeMay had prior experience of Bill Irvine's abilities and gave him wide latitude. However, when Irvine bypassed the chain of command, sending shipment requests directly with the materiel office in Ohio, Lieutenant General Robert C. Richardson, commanding army forces in the Central Pacific, was irate over the perceived insult. Somehow XXI Bomber Command was getting ships and aircraft bearing badly needed spare parts despite the irregularities. LeMay didn't care about ruffled feathers or protocol. He ignored the official protests and pointedly declined to ask Irvine any "stupid questions." It was an early indication of his willingness to run interference for productive subordinates—and far from the last.

Seven weeks after relieving Possum Hansell in the Marianas, LeMay saw no improvement over his predecessor's record. Under LeMay, XXI Bomber Command had launched more than a thousand sorties on eight missions but barely one-third of the aircraft had bombed the primary targets, none of which were destroyed. That galled LeMay, for whom target destruction was an obsession. It was, after all, the object of the exercise. He began wondering if high-altitude bombing could be as effective over Japan as over Germany.

Materiel and weather originally limited LeMay to a maximum of seven daylight missions per month, so he looked to radar as a means of expanding the operating window. However, he soon learned that there were few specially trained radar operators; most were gunners assigned the duty because there was little for them to do. Some could operate the equipment when it was working properly, but none could "tweak" the gear in flight. Radar bombing became, literally, a hit or miss proposition, and viable only when targets were clearly defined by land and sea.

The more LeMay learned about the situation, the more he felt that he needed flight time over Japan to assess his crews' limits, capabilities, and potential. He had gotten away with flying one mission in China but that was before he was told of a secret he called "the firecracker." Knowledge of the atomic bomb meant that Curtis LeMay had flown his last combat mission.

However, there were glints of improvement. Two February missions were dedicated incendiary raids: Kobe and Tokyo's urban industrial districts. They both produced impressive results, especially a Tokyo strike on February 25. Brigadier General Thomas S. Power, the egotistical yet competent leader of the newly arrived 314th Bomb Wing, speculated that low-level fire bombing could achieve even greater results. He discussed it with LeMay, who was characteristically receptive to subordinates' suggestions.

The main thing was to find a way around the atrocious weather, particularly the screaming winds aloft. Conditions over Japan resembled nothing seen elsewhere in the war. Flying at the doctrinal 30,000 feet, B-29s found astonishing winds—one of the first encounters with the jet stream. Consequently, accuracy evaporated. The Norden bomb sight was unable to compensate for the tremendous speeds often generated by tail winds, and the crosswind component was even worse. Nor was flying upwind the answer, as it could reduce the Superfort's 200-mph cruise speed by half or more.

Clearly, the answer lay in lower bombing altitudes, but that would put the Boeings in the heart of the light flak envelope. The operations analysts were appalled: They predicted 70 percent losses. What to do?

LeMay pondered a variety of options. Power and others at XXI Bomber Command supported the concept of low-level missions, but the idea extended farther afield. Dr. Edward L. Bowles, an MIT advisor to the War Department, had already posited low-level B-29 missions, but the radical approach had received little, if any, attention. Such a decision would rest with those in the theater of operations.[5]

Eventually LeMay decided to combine several innovations at once in preference to successive individual changes. Rather than flying "low" at 15,000 to 18,000 feet, he decided to send in his bombers at 5,000 to 9,000. Referring to his artillery tables as he had in England, he determined that Japanese gunners would be unable to track the bombers long enough to put up a useful barrage.

The primary risk was exposure to "the light stuff" that could chop up low-flying targets as big as B-29s. The trouble was, nobody knew how many light and medium-caliber anti-aircraft (AA) guns the Japanese actually had.

In addition to the seemingly suicidal low altitudes, LeMay added another change: He would launch his bombers against Tokyo at night. He was confident that darkness would offset the B-29s' potential vulnerability at lower altitudes, partly shielding the Boeings from AA observation. It was already known that Japan's night fighter force was almost nonexistent, and nowhere as capable of the Luftwaffe's Nachtjaeger, who could down scores of RAF bombers per mission.

Operating at night, at lower altitudes, offered numerous advantages. Extra fuel was unnecessary for the climb to 30,000 feet, and the balky Wright engines would perform better. Flying at night permitted LeMay to dispense with most of the B-29's formidable defensive armament, and the combined saving in fuel, guns, and ammunition amounted to more than four tons.

It was a calculated risk: A B-29 cost some $600,000—nearly three times a B-17—and losses already were heavier than Washington liked.

Deciding to gamble, in early March Curtis LeMay rolled the dice.

In opting for such a drastic change in tactics, LeMay was taking his professional life in his hands—an act of moral courage. While he never confused his personal fortunes with the lives of his aircrews or attainment of any mission, he knew the risk to his career. Norstad had told him as much: If LeMay failed, he would be fired.

Beyond the personal concerns, LeMay was literally flying in the face of the Army Air Force's most cherished dogma: Daylight, high-altitude, strategic bombing. If the low-level night mission flopped, his heretical decision to abandon military orthodoxy could cast him into professional outer darkness. After all, he knew what had happened to airmen who bucked the political currents: Billy Mitchell and Frank Andrews being prime examples of those whose careers suffered for speaking their minds.

LeMay's decision should be studied by current airmen and soldiers as an exercise in risk assessment, self confidence, and leadership. At rock bottom, it boiled down to the frontier wisdom of Davy Crockett: "Be sure you're right, then go ahead."

On the afternoon of March 9, 346 Boeings began lifting off their Marianas runways, a process that took two and a half hours. The 145th meridian led straight north from Guam, and Tokyo straddled the 140th. The target, therefore, bore five degrees west of north. LeMay watched Powers's wing take off that afternoon, then returned to headquarters for the long wait.

In a matter of hours one-sixth of the Japanese capital was burned to the ground. Power orbited overhead, providing running commentary of a catastrophe of greater proportions than the London fire of 1666, the destruction of Moscow in 1812, or the San Francisco earthquake of 1906. Observing the effects of 1,858 tons of incendiary chemicals, he summarized, "No other air attack of the war . . . was so destructive of life and property."[6]

On the ground, it was hell on earth. Subsequently the Tokyo fire chief admitted that his department lost control of the situation in half an hour; nearly one hundred fire engines were incinerated with their crews. The exact toll will never be known, but at least 83,000 people perished that night, and more than a quarter million buildings were destroyed. It was a disaster of stunning magnitude—thus far in the war Tokyo had lost fewer than 1,300 citizens.[7]

Overhead, the biggest planes in the world were tossed and thumped in bake-oven heat that forced B-29s upward 1,500 feet, then dropped them back into swirling, violent turbulence. Fourteen Boeings were lost, a 4 percent attrition rate.

Attending the debriefs was the Harvard statistician Robert S. McNamara, who had seen B-29 operations in China. To the tweedy number cruncher, LeMay was "monosyllabic, intolerant of criticism." Yet, when a pilot asked why his group sustained losses attacking from 5,000 feet, LeMay replied, "Why are we here?" It was a rhetorical question; he already knew the answer, adding, "Losses hurt me as much as you. But you lost one wingman and we destroyed Tokyo." McNamara was impressed not merely by the sentiment, but by the extent of the response. Much later he said it was the longest speech he ever heard LeMay deliver.[8]

LeMay harbored no doubts about the necessity of his command's actions. Typically blunt, he later wrote of the March 9 mission, "We scorched and boiled and baked to death more people in Tokyo . . . than went up in vapor at Hiroshima and Nagasaki combined." That was not quite true—some 80,000 perished in Hiroshima alone—but the sentiment was classic LeMay.[9]

After the March 9 scalding, LeMay possessed enough incendiaries for just four more fire raids. Consequently, XXI Bomber Command did what it could with high-explosive "iron bombs" until the navy delivered more shiploads of incendiaries.

Two nights after Tokyo burned, XXI Bomber Command launched 311 planes for Nagoya, Japan's third-largest city and center of the aircraft industry. As the bomber stream turned south for home, tail gunners could still see the red-orange glow of a burning city 150 miles away.

The next incendiary target was Osaka, attacked by 301 bombers on March 13. Over 90 percent reached the objective, bombing by radar through the undercast. Bombardiers used a technique called "offset aim point," directing their planes on a compass bearing from an identifiable radar target. The result, LeMay said, proved that Tokyo had been no fluke.[10]

In all, XXI Bomber Command conducted a ten-day "fire blitz," then ran out of ordnance. In just seven months, Tokyo's population was reduced by more than 50 percent, largely through evacuations.[11]

LeMay celebrated by treating himself to some Cuban cigars.

Subordinates said that LeMay never demonstrated any emotion about his work, let alone any remorse. He had a pragmatic attitude, focused on the technical aspects of logistics, maintenance, and operations. His ultimate statement on mass killing was, "Do you want to kill Japanese, or would you rather have Americans killed?"[12]

Despite his distant, impersonal image, and widely reported statements such as the foregoing, Curtis LeMay was not without his human side. He could envision a three-year-old girl screaming for her mother in a burning house. He could also switch off that image to focus upon ending the carnage.

LeMay was a professional soldier—an airman—whose government gave him a task that required killing large numbers of enemy civilians so the war could be won. The Strategic Bombing Survey concluded that 330,000 Japanese died in air attacks during 1944–45 and some half a million were injured, mostly by B-29s. However, LeMay was able to compartmentalize the horrific destruction that his command inflicted upon Japan. It was the price that nation-states paid for starting wars.

Curtis LeMay's main concern was to save lives: Those of his aircrews, not the enemy population. He was given the men, the aircraft, and the weapons with which to fight that war, and he accepted the responsibility with the tools provided. In fact, fire bombing Japan's largely wooden cities had been discussed before 1941, and a series of incendiaries began development even before LeMay went to Europe.

Contrary to the situation in Germany, where relatively few women entered the labor force, Japan truly was a nation under arms.

In the spring of 1945 most schools had closed to permit mobilization of males from fifteen to sixty and females from seventeen to forty. Additionally, Japan's war-making potential relied upon a "cottage industry" composed of small "feeder" businesses that often operated in homes or family shops, sending component parts to factories. LeMay especially noted the city of Yokohama where, emerging from the rubble, a forest of ruined drill presses and machine lathes stood in blackened testimony to the dispersal of Japanese military production.

Another factor in LeMay's choice of weapons and tactics was the inherent limitations of 1940s aviation technology. As the British had learned over Occupied Europe, it was extremely difficult to find a factory-sized target that devoutly wished to remain obscure. Consequently, the Royal Air Force attacked targets that it could find and strike: city centers. Radar helped simplify navigation and target identification, but it remained an immature technology into 1945, and could not reliably put bombs within 1,000 feet of the aim point. Therefore, LeMay, like his RAF counterpart Sir Arthur Harris, fought the only kind of battle that he could: area attacks against large cities.

Consequently, the best way to destroy enemy industry was to attack urban areas. From a professional viewpoint, LeMay can be faulted for pursuing Hansell's failed policy of high-altitude bombing as long as he did. But when he recognized that the conventional wisdom did not apply over Japan, with extremely high winds and frequent poor weather, he did what he had to do. He got on with ending the war.

Destroying the enemy was not only a matter of moving ordnance. LeMay determined that the optimum use of his fliers and bombers was 80 hours a month per crew (five or six missions) and 120 per airplane. Consequently, his staff was able to allocate assets to each mission with ever greater efficiency. By spring, XXI Bomber Command was operating with the practiced routine of a well-run airline. The difference, of course, was that the airplanes destroyed whatever city was their destination.

In the twenty-first century, no direct comparison can be made with the massive bombing missions of the 1940s. Today, when the goal is to minimize casualties and use far fewer bombers with precision guided munitions, strategic airpower has lost much of its separate identity. "Strategic bombers" can be any aircraft capable of carrying a nuclear weapon, but strategic goals now are routinely met by individual airplanes putting laser or electro-optically guided ordnance through the desired window of a power plant or command bunker.

LeMay would approve of recent technological evolution not only for its greater efficiency but for the reduced risk to American and allied aircrews. With ever greater "standoff" capability, launching weapons from longer distances, the airpower millennium surely has arrived.

But still there are critics. During the 1999 NATO operation in Yugoslavia, a high-altitude bomb aimed at a bridge destroyed a railroad car, causing at least ten civilian deaths. In another instance the Chinese embassy in Belgrade was struck in a targeting error. The news media reported a flurry of outraged responses from around the globe, but LeMay probably would have observed that the combined death toll from those incidents barely equaled the crew of one B-29.

+≡≡+

When Boeing designed the B-29, no one expected the huge bomber to deliver mines against enemy convoy routes. But the concept had been tested and proven before LeMay arrived in China. In August 1944 the first very long-range mining mission was flown against the petroleum-producing area of the Dutch East Indies. Staging through Ceylon, the XX Bomber Command crews logged an incredible 4,000-mile round trip, demonstrating the increasing reach of American airpower.

Knowing the Twentieth Air Force's potential, Admiral Ernest J. King in Washington prevailed upon the joint chiefs to commit

B-29s to mining operations. Consequently, the Central Pacific commander, Admiral Chester Nimitz, approached LeMay about a large-scale campaign in Japan's home islands. It took little persuasion, as the bomber chief recognized the potential of the Clausewitzian concept of economy of force: maximum results for minimal effort. With XXI Bomber Command growing almost month by month, it could afford to divert thirty or so planes per night to supporting the naval war.

Beginning "Operation Starvation" in late March, Brigadier General John H. Davies' 313th Bomb Wing sowed a thousand mines in high density patterns calculated to prevent effective sweeping by the Japanese. The figure doubled in April and mining continued unabated. Most Japanese ports and obvious choke points such as straits were mined and restocked at frequent intervals, with defensive measures further complicated by a variety of detonators: Magnetic, acoustic, and pressure.

LeMay allotted his "miners" carefully, with an eye toward efficiency. In forty-six missions, the '29s delivered more than 12,000 mines, losing fifteen planes while depriving Tokyo of 1,250,000 tons of increasingly rare merchant shipping. Yet the 1,500 mining sorties represented less than 6 percent of XXI Bomber Command overall effort.

The B-29 operation was enormously successful: By May 1945 the campaign was sinking nearly three ships a day. Postwar analysts found that three-quarters of the most important convoy routes had been closed, and Operation Starvation accounted for more results—670 ships sunk and damaged—than all other causes combined.

LeMay's B-29 fleet continued to grow. Beginning in February, XXI Bomber Command received one new wing per month, including the Fifty-Eighth from India in March. With arrival of Brigadier General Frank Armstrong's 315th in early April, LeMay's strength peaked at five wings with twenty groups: eighty squadrons of the world's most capable bomber. Yet for coordination and the kind of hands-on leadership he preferred, LeMay could not easily visit his commands, since the wings were dispersed on three islands 135 miles apart: one on Saipan, two each on Guam and Tinian. With his headquarters on Guam, LeMay could only access the 314th and 315th on North and Northwest Fields, without flying to the other islands.

Though a relative Pacific latecomer, Armstrong exerted a profound effect upon the B-29 campaign. He was well known to LeMay from a navigation course a decade previously and had welcomed the 305th Group to England in 1942. LeMay considered him "an old warhorse" (he was 43) and an astute airman. The 315th Wing immediately proved its worth with precision radar attacks against Japanese oil targets, thanks to the four groups' Eagle radar, optimized for bombing rather than navigation.

In a matter of a few months the B-29s' ability to raze urban Japan was only limited by the navy's ability to deliver fuel and ordnance. The Japanese came to know LeMay by name and reputation. Reportedly he was called Kikhiku Rumei, variously interpreted as "monster" or "beast."

April 1, 1945, was both Easter and April Fool's Day. It was also L-Day for Operation Iceberg, the invasion of Okinawa, the largest island south of Japan. Prior to the landings, XXI Bomber Command had pounded Japanese airfields on Kyushu, and LeMay reckoned his bombers had done enough to support the navy. He asked permission of Admiral Nimitz, the theater commander, to return to strategic targets but was denied. Kyushu's kamikaze bases continued sprouting their lethal eggs, and the B-29s were tasked with more prophylactic action. The campaign continued until May 11, when the Twentieth Air Force finally received Nimitz's heartfelt thanks. LeMay chewed his cigar in quiet frustration: the '29 was not a tactical aircraft, and he felt it had been misused.

With Nimitz's approval to return to attacking Japanese industry, LeMay resumed fire raids on May 14 with a daylight blitz that left Nagoya's aircraft engine plant in ruins and more than three square miles of the city in rubble. Returning the next night, the B-29s attacked with even greater ferocity from low level, burning nearly four more square miles of urban area to the ground.

At 5:00 A.M. on April 13, LeMay was awakened by a staff officer asking if XXI Bomber Command had any Medals of Honor. The day before, B-29 gunner Henry Erwin had been dropping markers through the chute in his aircraft when one of the devices ignited. His face was seared and he reeled backward, blinded and gasping. Blazing with magnesium intensity, the flare fell to the floor, spewing thick, choking smoke through the bomber. Somehow, Erwin picked up the blazing flare and tossed it overboard before collapsing. His awesome courage was judged worthy of the Medal of Honor, and XXI Bomber Command officers wanted LeMay's approval to begin the process. They immediately received it.

Hap Arnold's office cleared the way, approving immediate presentation while Erwin still lived. However, learning that no Medals of Honor were available, LeMay dispatched a plane to Hawaii with orders to fetch back a "Congressional" medal by any means. Arriving after hours, the fliers broke into a display case at Honolulu headquarters, stole the decoration, and returned to Guam.

Only a week after the action, LeMay stood by the twenty-three-year-old hero's bedside and presented America's highest decoration for valor. With typical understatement the general said, "Your effort to save the lives of your fellow airmen is the most extraordinary kind of heroism I know."

Swathed in bandages and ointment, "Red" Erwin merely drawled, "Thank you, sir." The Alabaman received the only Medal of Honor awarded in the Twentieth Air Force—and lived another fifty-six years.

+=====+

In late May 1945 an unusual organization began arriving on Tinian, eighty-five miles north of Guam. It was the 509th Composite Group, composed of just one bomb squadron and a transport squadron plus supporting units. Its commander was Lieutenant Colonel Paul W. Tibbets, with a wealth of experience in Europe and North Africa.

After suggesting that the 509th sharpen its shooting eye against nearby Rota—an island left in Japanese hands—LeMay said, "Paul, I want you to understand one thing: no flying for you over the empire." Tibbets instantly knew why—the secret of the atomic "firecracker" would be imperiled if he were captured—and saluted smartly. Then he began looking for a way around Curt LeMay's order.[13]

LeMay, the thirty-eight-year-old general, and Tibbets, the twenty-nine-year-old mission commander, now held more raw power and responsibility than most presidents and prime ministers.

In Europe, LeMay had flown missions with as many as sixty B-17s shot down at a time. Even half that loss rate would end the B-29 campaign in the Pacific, and he kept his finger on the pulse of his force, seeking every means of reducing aircrew casualties. He found that with its enormous complexity, the B-29 was its own worst enemy.

From January through August, XXI Bomber Command lost 309 B-29s to all causes, of which enemy action represented barely one third. By far the worst month was May, with eighty-eight losses, of which a whopping sixty-five were accidental. In only one other month (April) did the toll exceed fifty. Monthly noncombat losses ranged between 40 and 80 percent of the total, averaging 63 percent in the last eight months of hostilities.[14]

By refining procedures and tactics, LeMay and his staff systematically pared losses until the world's most complex bomber was operating with unprecedented efficiency. During July—the last full month of hostilities—XXI Bomber Command was running massive operations with airline regularity. On nine nights that month, LeMay launched major efforts totaling nearly 4,800 bombing and mining sorties, plus smaller missions. On average the command put up 527 bombers per night, usually 100 to 125 aircraft per wing. Losses were sustainable: only eighteen B-29s lost to all causes that month. In fact, on July 24, all 660 Superfortresses returned to base.

Hap Arnold's health remained precarious but he recovered enough to visit the Marianas during a Pacific inspection tour in June 1945, consulting with XXI Bomber Command staff on Saipan. The air chief was received by Lieutenant General Barney Giles, commanding the Pacific Air Forces, with LeMay and Rosey O'Donnell. Arnold then proceeded to Guam, where he could frankly discuss matters five stars to five stars with Fleet Admiral Nimitz. As commander of Twentieth Air Force, Arnold knew of "the bomb problem" that LeMay had raised with Nimitz: deliveries and handling being sore points. From both an operational and institutional perspective, LeMay felt hamstrung in that the navy theater commander held de facto veto power over B-29 operations based on how much shipping was allocated to supporting XXI Bomber Command. Hap Arnold and Chet Nimitz thrashed things out, and LeMay got on with the war.[15]

During further discussions with Arnold, LeMay predicted that he would exhaust his target list around the first of September. That assessment, of course, did not account for the atomic bombs, but clearly additional planning was called for. Consequently, LeMay strapped into the left seat of a B-29 and headed for Washington on June 15. The 8,500-mile trip was made in record time with the general making all takeoffs and landings.

While Helen scrambled to meet her long-absent husband, LeMay briefed the joint chiefs on B-29 operations. As LeMay's briefing officers conducted a polished presentation, their chief noticed that General of the Army George Marshall had fallen asleep in his chair. Recognizing that continuing the presentation was useless, the Marianas airmen folded their papers and withdrew. The service chiefs seemed convinced that an invasion was necessary, and presumably XXI Bomber Command was overly confident of its ability to force Tokyo's capitulation. Before the long, long flight west, LeMay talked to Major General Leslie Groves, who ran the Manhattan Project. He told LeMay to expect the first "special weapon" at the end of July and recommended using each weapon as it arrived.

Meanwhile, conventional bombing was destroying Japanese cities almost every night. But LeMay's staff found a way to accelerate the civilian exodus from targeted areas. The navy had been providing leaflets urging Japanese to vacate their homes, but there was little evidence that the warnings were heeded. LeMay reckoned that XXI Bomber Command could do better and ordered an ominous looking flyer printed with red and black ink. On one side it urged civilians to leave at once. On the other was printed more specific information in Japanese: "These leaflets are being dropped to notify you that your city has been listed for destruction by our powerful air force. The bombing will begin within seventy-two hours." It went on to state that Japan's armed forces were powerless to prevent aerial annihilation.

Ironically, the Japanese government had already tried to evacuate Tokyo residents not employed in factories or other war-related work. As far back as October 1943 the war cabinet had urged such departures, but most citizens resisted. Eventually hundreds of thousands of children were moved to outlying or rural areas, and as "B-san" (B-29s) appeared more often, other residents also departed. By March 1945, mainly through evacuations, the capital's population had dropped from nearly seven million to roughly five million, including the aged, war workers, and infants.[16]

Those figures do not mean that XXI Bomber Command was responsible for some two million deaths. Rather, it was the total reduction in Tokyo's population by all causes, mainly evacuation. It has already been noted that total Japanese deaths by aerial bombardment were about 330,000.

At first the air force leaflets yielded no better results than the navy versions. But after the first three cities were leveled, the others were largely depopulated, as LeMay said, "in nothing flat."[17]

In July and August, Twentieth Air Force headquarters moved from Washington, D.C., to Guam. Consequently, LeMay officially lost his position because Headquarters XXI Bomber Command was redesignated Headquarters Twentieth Air Force, now under Lieutenant General Nathan Twining. However, the wings continued operating as before, still directed by LeMay, so little actually changed. LeMay, officially chief of staff to General Carl Spaatz, running the new Strategic Air Forces, remained a two-star.

If LeMay gave one moment's thought to matters of rank and seniority, he never voiced them. Most likely he was far too absorbed in the continuing effort to wrest the last pound of fuel, ordnance, and human efficiency from his command.

And efficient it was, even in comparison to other Allied efforts. By July and August the Twentieth Air Force was launching 600 to 700 B-29s per day or night. In comparison, on April 4–5, Royal Air Force Bomber Command had mounted a Herculean effort with 1,172 sorties including small, twin-engine DeHavilland Mosquitoes. On eight other missions that month the British put up 500 to 900 bombers, but the median figure for the last full month of the European war was barely 200 Bomber Command sorties, again including Mosquitoes. Whatever the numbers, the second largest Allied air force could not match the awesome weight of most B-29 operations.

It became increasingly clear: Curtis LeMay commanded the most potent air force on the planet.

On August 2, LeMay flew to Tinian to brief the 509th Composite Group on an operation called Special Mission Number 13. The group commander, Paul Tibbets, had already drafted the body of the operations order; now LeMay filled in the blanks.

The mission date was four days hence—Monday, August 6. The three possible targets were Hiroshima as the primary, Kokura as secondary, and Nagasaki as backup. Hiroshima was the obvious first choice: It was the army area headquarters for the defense of Kyushu, Japan's southernmost island, and therefore figured prominently in the planned invasion slated for November. Ironically, it was home of the Japanese army's submarine school. While no other army likely operated its own submarines, Tokyo's general staff enacted the measure to supply bypassed island garrisons.

After the briefing, Tibbets escorted LeMay to the armament area for a look at the uranium "firecracker". LeMay eyed the rotund shape called Little Boy, wished the 509th the best of luck, and returned to Guam.

＋——·——＋

In the predawn Monday blackness of August 6, a twenty-nine-year-old pilot firewalled the throttles of the B-29 known as "Dimples 82." But that was merely the radio callsign; the world would remember her as *Enola Gay*. Two other Superfortresses accompanied her from Tinian, monitoring the effects of her unique ordnance upon Japan's seventh largest city, Hiroshima.

Twelve hours and thirteen minutes later, *Enola Gay* returned to roost. In that time the Army Air Forces, the war, and the world were irrevocably changed. "Little Boy," a uranium bomb of some fifteen megatons, had performed as intended.

The next day, LeMay studied post-strike photography of the ruined city. He was unexpectedly surprised at the extent of devastation but otherwise expressed little if any concern for future implications. Curtis LeMay was far too astute to regard the atomic bomb as merely an exceptionally large weapon, and perhaps he grasped that his professional future would be intimately tied to nuclear weapons. But his unemotional reaction to Little Boy's stunning performance was likely a combination of his normal sangfroid and his absorption with running his part of the war. A mission had been flown successfully; more missions lay ahead.

In context of the time, there was no immediate reason for LeMay or other Army Air Forces leaders to worry over future implications of atomic weapons. America was the world's only nuclear power, and that month she possessed only one other bomb. Plans were discussed for possible use of A-bombs in the invasion of Japan beginning in November, but that contingency would await word from Washington. For the moment, Russia loomed as a probable postwar adversary, but only later would the extent of Soviet infiltration of the U.S. bomb program be known.

After Hiroshima there was no respite for Twentieth Air Force crews, who struck four Japanese cities on the seventh and eighth. One-fifth of Yawata was burned down; so was nearly three-quarters of Fukuyama.

Nagasaki had been attacked occasionally by B-24s and medium bombers from Okinawa, but not by B-29s. As a major industrial and shipbuilding center, it made the "short list" of prospective atomic targets, and, absent any sign of capitulation from Tokyo, it was leveled by the plutonium weapon called "Fat Man" on August 9.

LeMay held absolutely no regrets about his role in inaugurating nuclear weapons to combat. "I did not and do not decry the use of the bomb," he wrote twenty years later. He believed that if atom bombs shortened the war only by a few days, the immense American effort and heavy Japanese toll were preferable to a sanguinary invasion. The "strange, pervading fear" that nuclear weapons produced in some humans was unwarranted in his opinion because there was nothing new in deaths caused by military forces.[18]

In the six decades since LeMay oversaw the only combat use of atomic bombs, their employment has become less likely by nation-states. However, in the era of terrorism and other weapons of mass destruction, the risk of devastation of a sort approaching Japan in 1945 cannot be dismissed out of hand. If there is a corollary between then and now, it will be found not in the use of weapons or technology, but in the capacity of leaders to adapt to shifting dynamics and paradigms. In that regard, LeMay offers some lessons:

He inherited an immature technology—the long-range bomber—and helped bring it to technical and tactical maturity. Furthermore, he received an enormously powerful weapon unlike any that existed before, and directed its effective use. He did both in an astonishingly short period: a few years for the bomber; a few weeks for the atomic weapon.

How LeMay adapted to such rapid, unprecedented changes merits close attention. His bedrock traits—thoroughness, mental agility, and self-confidence—paved the potentially rocky road to success.

Certainly LeMay's colleagues and superiors admired his unexcelled competence. After a close look at the "Baker 29" (B-29) operation, General Carl Spaatz of the Pacific Strategic Air Forces called LeMay's command "the best organized and most technically and tactically proficient military organization the world has seen to date." That assessment was dated August 7, the day after Hiroshima.

Meanwhile, operations continued against an implacable enemy. Seventy conventional firebirds returned to Tokyo on August 10—the small force was judged adequate to the task—while others continued mining operations. LeMay's earlier estimate that he would run out of worthwhile targets by September was looking slightly conservative. Anticipating Japan's capitulation, President Truman grounded the Twentieth Air Force during the next three days.

With no word from Tokyo, on August 14 LeMay sent 752 Superforts winging north on seven missions, returning without loss. The eighty-one bombers over Kumagaya reduced nearly half the city to ashes. Other aerial task forces attacked army and navy arsenals, petroleum, and transport targets. Before the attackers landed, the war was over.

The emperor publicly announced Japan's surrender on August 15, with news reaching LeMay's command after dinner. For a few minutes the Guamanian night air was rent by happy shouts, celebratory gunfire, and a general scurrying about. But LeMay and his staff were surprised at how quickly the celebration died down. Before long, lights were doused and the island descended into unaccustomed quiet: no urgent maintenance; no hasty bomb loading; just time to sleep.

+═══+

As one of the Allied commanders who defeated Imperial Japan, LeMay was invited to attend the formal surrender. He flew a Douglas C-54 transport into Yokohama in time for the September 2 ceremony in Tokyo Bay, standing with other Allied commanders aboard the battleship *Missouri.* As dignified Japanese gentlemen signed the documents, LeMay mused upon the thousands of airmen who had purchased that moment at the expense of their lives. And briefly he wondered how he might have done his duty more efficiently to spare a few more of those youngsters.

If at that moment he gave any thought to the Japanese dead, LeMay never recorded it. Had anyone asked him, he might have replied that they had the misfortune to be born in an aggressive, expansionist nation that worshipped a living deity and lauded death in his service. That tens of thousands had died in view of the Imperial Palace for nine months said more about the emperor's warlords than it did about those who toppled his regime.

Then General Douglas MacArthur said, "These proceedings are closed," and the Tokyo sky churned with the resonant chorus of 1,848 Cyclone engines propelling 462 Superfortresses overhead.

LeMay later said that he stood immobile, watching the aerial procession, feeling little more than fatigue. But his professional curiosity soon roused him. Reboarding his C-54, he conducted a low-level tour of most major Japanese cities, observing firsthand the effects of his bombers' handiwork. Satisfied with the work his fliers had accomplished, he eased the Douglas into a southerly bank, headed for Guam.

Barely two weeks after the surrender, Arnold asked for a three-plane B-29 formation from Tokyo to Washington, demonstrating the Superfort's immense range to the public. However, no Japanese airfield could accommodate the 71-ton weight necessary so the mission launched from Guam. In B-29s fitted with long-range tanks, LeMay, Barney Giles, and Rosey O'Donnell stretched the fuel to Chicago before proceeding onward to D.C.

The war was truly over.

CHAPTER 6

Postwar

FOLLOWING THEIR LONG-RANGE FORMATION FLIGHT FROM Japan in September 1945, LeMay and Rosey O'Donnell reported to General Carl Spaatz in Washington. As Arnold's successor to command the Army Air Forces, "Tooey" Spaatz was pulled in two directions: dismantling the greatest assembly of airpower ever conceived, and continuing technical development at the dawn of the jet age.

The generals pondered their options and decided that O'Donnell would conduct the onerous staff work in D.C. while LeMay would pursue the technical end at Wright Field near Dayton.

The assignment pleased the LeMays; Helen also was a native Ohioan, and the Air Materiel Command was bound to keep pace with the latest developments.

However, the family had barely settled near Dayton when Spaatz changed his mind. O'Donnell was sent to Wright Field and

LeMay was recalled to D.C.; his new title was deputy chief of air staff for research and development (R&D).

Though he likely did not know it, the R&D position represented a significant compliment to LeMay's ability. In considering candidates, the board established by Spaatz specifically had recommended "an officer of the caliber of Curtis E. LeMay."[1]

LeMay dreaded the Washington assignment. Never one to enjoy socializing, he knew the inevitable obligations attending a two-star general in the nation's capitol, and accepted his fate with typical stoicism. (He was known to sit through an entire dinner party without speaking a word, even if he knew his dining companions.)

Reluctantly, LeMay settled behind his desk in the "Big House," as he called the Pentagon. While he learned the R&D trade, the simmering battle over an independent air force quickly burst its wartime seams. The Army Air Forces had proven their worth—partly thanks to Major General LeMay—and the airmen recognized a priceless opportunity.

The battle for a separate air arm was fought on several fronts: in Congress, in the press, and in the public mind. The Armed Forces Unification Act was built on two premises: a department of defense with a civilian secretary wielding authority over the service secretaries and chiefs; and an independent air force. The navy was bitterly opposed to the concept. Though naval aviation had been indispensable to defeating Japan, the golden-winged admirals feared that a new air force would seek to take roles and missions currently in their domain.

They were right.

Meanwhile, LeMay began educating himself about the R&D world. He knew how little research had been conducted before the war, and was surprised to learn how progressive the Germans had been from the 1930s through 1945. They led the world in jet propulsion and had rocketry almost to themselves. Their theoretical and practical knowledge of high speed flight was such that the

United States, Britain, and Russia all scrambled to scoop up German data, engineers, and scientists.

LeMay knew that the American effort differed from the Soviet in that no Germans were brought to the United States against their will. But his command had responsibility for Project Paper Clip, recruiting German scientists and engineers such as Doctor Werner von Braun and General Walter Dornberger, the leading minds behind the V-2 rocket program.

Though he had arisen to prominence on reciprocating engines, LeMay recognized the immense potential of new propulsion systems. But apart from jets and rockets, he was also receptive to other innovations such as satellites. LeMay's scientific consultants convinced him that it was possible to place a satellite in earth orbit, but in 1946 the cost would have been astronomical. Amid the greatest downsizing in military history, millions for space exploration were simply not a political reality.

Meanwhile, LeMay learned a great deal about politics, reality, and the view from Capitol Hill. He likened his first Washington stint to a siege, with repeated appearances before congressional committees, testifying about the need for greater research funding. Without quite realizing it, he was laying the foundation for his extraordinary success over the next twenty years, winning converts and reinforcing alliances among the politicians who controlled the air arm's budgets.

Ironically, LeMay almost received a free ticket into politics while serving in Washington. The ink had barely dried in Tokyo Bay when a vacancy occurred in the U.S. Senate as an Ohio politician was appointed to the Supreme Court. The state's governor was required to appoint an occupant for the unexpired term and LeMay, being a native son, was offered the position. He seriously considered it until he learned that he would have to resign his commission. The law permitted commissioned officers to sit in Congress but not in the Senate.

As biographer Thomas M. Coffey noted, Governor Frank Lausche was a conservative Democrat and apparently felt that LeMay was a kindred soul, though of the Republican variety. Just how conservative the general truly was had not yet become apparent, but his political philosophy had been molded from childhood and was impervious to alteration. Fiercely independent and self-reliant—to an extent self-educated—he became the chilliest of cold war Republicans.[2]

Despite his cordial relations with Mao's forces in China, LeMay was increasingly focused on the growing Communist threat, especially from Russia. In that context, he was appointed to chair a Joint Chiefs subcommittee on nuclear testing that completed its suggestions before the end of 1945. In June 1946 he traveled to the Pacific to witness his first nuclear detonation. For Operation Crossroads he flew to the Marshall Islands where one of his R&D B-29s was assigned to drop a weapon at Bikini Atoll. Test Able, which captured global news coverage (by one reckoning half the world supply of movie film was on hand), produced some twenty-three kilotons: roughly the yield of the "Fat Man" bomb at Nagasaki.

However, LeMay's bomber crew had missed the target by a third of a mile. Test Baker occurred a month later, a similar weapon detonated under water.

By that time LeMay recognized a serious deficiency in the Army Air Force's nuclear capability. Dating from before Hiroshima, the AAF had merely been a delivery system for atomic bombs; very few personnel knew anything about the Manhattan Project's inner workings. In March 1946 LeMay had approached Major General Frederick L. Anderson, assistant chief for personnel, urging that the air force develop the ability to maintain and handle nuclear weapons. General Ira Eaker, deputy chief of staff, saw the merit and directed Anderson to assist LeMay in selecting sufficient numbers of qualified personnel.[3]

The process was predictably slow. That summer only ten officers had been trained as "weaponeers" but more had been selected, and LeMay's vision would yield greater results.

Later that year, despite his R&D obligations, LeMay was back in the operational realm. In the spring of 1946 the air staff began drafting Makefast, a plan for commitment of air force units at the outbreak of hostilities. Based on the demonstrated success of the European air offensive, it targeted the Soviet oil industry with conventional bombers. Upon completion in October it was handed to LeMay for his recommendations as to how nuclear weapons should be integrated into the overall plan.[4]

⊹⇒═⇐⊹

Curt LeMay got drunk on the night of July 26, 1947.

It was not the first time he had tied one on, but it was damned rare. For a man as rigidly self-controlled as LeMay, to cut loose was almost unheard of.

On that day, aboard the presidential aircraft called *The Sacred Cow*, Harry Truman had signed the National Security Act establishing a Department of Defense and, with it, an independent U.S. Air Force.

Though the act did not take effect until September, it was widely reported that far, far above the contrail level the shades of Billy Mitchell and Bob Olds undoubtedly joined LeMay and a generation of airmen by hoisting a heavenly brew.

Further cause for celebration was close at hand. On October 1 LeMay was elevated to lieutenant general, making him the youngest three-star in the service. His new post was commander of U.S. Air Forces in Europe (USAFE), headquartered in Germany. The irony could not have escaped him: The last time he had flown into German airspace had been at the head of hundreds of B-17s. Now he was charged with defending West Germany, and the rest of free Europe, from the looming Soviet specter.

LeMay took over from a West Pointer, Brigadier General John F. McBlain, who was several years senior to LeMay. An engineering and staff officer, McBlain had been USAFE's interim commander for two months.

The LeMays moved into their new home at Wiesbaden, west of Frankfurt, marveling at the ambience: The U.S. military had long since appropriated the huge mansion of a former champagne dealer with ties to the Nazi regime. With more than 100 rooms, the usual staff involved nearly forty servants but the economy-minded LeMays managed with eighteen.[5]

From the general's perspective there were three salient problems: The Russians pouting only seventy-five miles to the east; a grossly understrength air force rapidly approaching obsolescence; and social obligations three or four times a week. Helen handled the latter chore with customary aplomb while nine-year-old Janie made friends with the domestic staff.

At the same time LeMay got acquainted with his professional staff. Characteristically, he established an open-door policy, noting that if he were busy at any moment he would throw the interlopers out.

Apart from his USAFE command, LeMay also was concerned with coordinating allied plans with the British and French. Because Germany was divided into occupation zones, the liaison chores were more complex than he would have preferred, but international cooperation was essential in the face of the Russian forces.

LeMay was nothing if not a pragmatist. With only eleven operational combat groups (and twenty-seven in caretaker or paper status), the U.S. Air Force could not hope to mount a rapid response to serious aggression anywhere on earth. USAFE's share of the paltry force structure made LeMay even more reliant upon whatever strength his allies could provide him.

The Soviets did nothing to alleviate LeMay's concerns. Toward year end, relations with Moscow degenerated, largely over continuing demands for war reparations from West Germany. The eastern part of the nation, of course, lay under the Russian heel, where it would remain for the next four decades. Generals Carl Spaatz and Hoyt S. Vandenberg, his vice chief of staff, made an inspection trip of Europe and, in event of hostilities, promised LeMay all the support they could muster. However well intended the pledge, none of the officers believed that USAFE could defeat a determined Communist offensive without resort to nuclear weapons. (As LeMay learned later that year, America's atomic capability was a necessarily well-kept secret, since the new Strategic Air Command constituted a hollow force.)

The new year of 1948 began no better. In February, Czech Communists overthrew the democratically elected government in Prague, adding to the continuing diplomatic feuds between Moscow and the West. The next month the Soviets left a meeting of the occupying powers, irate over an Anglo-American plan to combine their economic aid to the western portions of Berlin.

In early April LeMay received a call from Army General Lucius D. Clay, U.S. military governor in Germany. The Russians, demonstrating de facto control of all external access to the capitol, were implementing oppressively bureaucratic requirements for inspection and certification of all rail and road shipments originating in West Germany. Clay asked if USAFE could provide Berlin with coal and perhaps some other supplies.

LeMay's pragmatic response was to ask how much coal was needed. At that early juncture, Clay merely wanted to demonstrate to Moscow that the Western powers would not be intimidated, so any cargo flights would suffice. LeMay had an immediate answer: He said that a C-47 group would ferry as much bagged coal as could be delivered to Rhine-Main Airport at nearby Frankfort.

Thus was born the "LeMay Coal and Feed Company."[6]

LeMay began thinking ahead of the game, anticipating the likely Soviet response. He knew that if ground transport were cut off, only an air bridge could keep West Berlin supplied, especially during a European winter. If the Russians wanted to prevent cargo flights into the zone, they could certainly do so by shooting down cargo planes. Consequently, LeMay alerted his best combat commander, Colonel Clarence T. Edwinson of the P-47 equipped Twenty-seventh Fighter Group.

"Curly" Edwinson had experience with the Russians. As commander of a Fifteenth Air Force fighter group in 1944, he had attacked a Soviet mechanized column in Yugoslavia, believing it was a German unit. The Russians, ever secretive, had declined to inform their allies of their progress, hence the error. Yak fighters intervened and the Lockheed P-38 pilots defended themselves, resulting in losses on both sides. The Communists were furious, demanding that the responsible American be executed. With a wink and a nod, Edwinson had been hastily "transferred" stateside. The incident had no effect on his career, as he enjoyed three subsequent commands and became a brigadier general.

At first it appeared that LeMay's efforts bore fruit. Despite the meager amounts of coal the C-47s could deliver, the Russians eased the new "regulations" and surface traffic resumed as before. Nevertheless, LeMay called for reinforcements and received twenty-eight B-29s from Smoky Hill Air Force Base in Kansas. None were nuclear capable, but the arrival of heavy bombers in the theater at least represented some resolve. LeMay ordered them to Britain, beyond reach of a Soviet surprise attack.

There followed a tentative thaw in the frosty European atmosphere, with the Russians alternatively approving and stopping road or rail traffic to Berlin. Diplomatic notes were exchanged, accusations were traded, and both sides prepared for a fight.

On June 22 the Russians ended all road and rail access to Berlin.

Apart from Curly Edwinson's fighter group and the UK-based B-29s, LeMay had other irons in the fire. He put his two transport groups on alert, informing them that they may have to conduct full-scale operations through contested airspace. He also consulted with an army counterpart, Major General Arthur G. Trudeau of the U.S. constabulary in Germany. The two commanders thought alike: Present a show of force and compel the Russians to back down. A lead-from-the-front officer much like LeMay, Trudeau proposed forcing a mechanized convoy through the Russian lines, watching for the enemy reaction while riding in the first truck. Any serious opposition would trigger LeMay's response, attacking Soviet radar sites and airfields with his available airpower.

General Clay expressed his thanks for the staff work, politely declining the combined army-air force plan. At least part of the reason for refusing the confrontational approach was due to allied sensibilities. LeMay and Trudeau knew full well that neither the French nor Belgians would permit allied troops on their soil without specific permission, and neither Paris nor Brussels would condone a de facto invasion of Soviet territory.

With surface transport blocked indefinitely, Clay turned to USAFE for a round-the-clock airlift. LeMay immediately realized that European assets were nowhere near adequate for so great an undertaking, and flatly said so. There were probably not enough C-47s in the air force to supply Berlin on the scale required, so LeMay began campaigning for all the four-engine transports in the U.S. inventory. Mainly, that meant Douglas C-54s.

The interim commander of the Berlin Airlift was Brigadier General Joseph Smith, the Wiesbaden area commander. The airlift, which Smith dubbed "Operation Vittles," began on June 26, four days after the blockade, with thirty-two flights delivering eighty tons of food and supplies.

Smith was a capable leader—he had served most of the war as a general staff officer and presidential aide—but LeMay needed airlift expertise. He knew exactly whom he needed: Major General William H. Tunner.

LeMay said that if you wanted to get the circus on the road, you called Mr. Ringling, the circus master. The same applied to Bill Tunner, "Mr. Airlift." He had turned the flights over "the Hump" from India into China into a roaring success, despite the most rugged terrain and some of the worst weather on earth. If anyone could keep Berlin fed, Tunner was the man. LeMay entrusted the details of Operation Vittles wholly to his capable hands and was not disappointed. Tunner and his British deputy, Air Commodore J. W. F. Mercer, produced ever-greater results.

However, LeMay was never content to stay behind when there was flying to be done. No longer encumbered by the security concerns he had endured on Guam, he felt free to deliver some goods to Berlin himself. Officially he was observing the efficiency of the operation, but the plain fact was that he enjoyed having altitude beneath him and a mission to complete.

Taking nothing away from Tunner's expertise, LeMay personally saw ways to improve the airlift's efficiency. He missed very little. He noted aircrews going for coffee or walking back and forth between the flight line and operations office and told his staff that they were going to "get smart." By having coffee, sandwiches, and ops officers near the parking areas, as much as half an hour could be shaved off a plane's turnaround time.

Despite the growing efficacy of Operation Vittles, LeMay was chronically short of one invaluable commodity: people. There simply were not enough men in the new blue uniform to support the airlift's myriad requirements: mechanics, cooks, and cargo handlers to name a few. Consequently, LeMay looked for the nearest source of manpower and found himself swimming in a sea of untapped potential. He hired Germans, thousands of them.

Few of the locals spoke English but there were enough translators and bilingual Americans and Germans to suffice. Besides, LeMay pragmatically concluded, nobody had to talk in order to toss a bag of coal into an airplane.

One of the greatest benefits was hiring former Luftwaffe mechanics. Despite the difference in metric and English tools, the principles were the same, and anyone who could replace pistons in a Daimler-Benz 605 could do the same in a Pratt and Whitney R1830. The Americans found that, apart from the satisfaction of working on aircraft again, the Germans were personally motivated to "keep 'em flying." Those who did not have family members in

Berlin still felt a *volkische* kinship with two and a half million fellow Germans.

Britain and France also contributed to the airlift, though in far smaller numbers. The RAF's peacetime structure was pitifully short on transports but the British obtained civil aircraft to fly into Berlin as well. Additionally, in the pre-NATO era, allied cooperation in Europe was more difficult to arrange than today, when multinational operations are largely taken for granted.

Before long, LeMay and Tunner recognized that the long-term nature of the airlift would require more than the air force could provide. Consequently, Naval Air Transport Command began sending heavy-lift Douglas R5C squadrons to Europe. It was a massive effort: At the peak of the operation in early 1949, 225 of the Skymasters were involved. The peak performance occurred on April 16, when nearly 1,400 sorties unloaded almost 13,000 tons in Berlin.

The Russians never tried to stop the airlift—they knew such action likely would lead to war—but their fighters occasionally harassed Vittles flights by buzzing the transports. Though there were reports of firing incidents, nothing came of them, so LeMay never had to call upon Curly Edwinson's Thunderbolt squadrons.

LeMay and Tunner saw Operation Vittles as a growth industry, capable of delivering even more than it was doing six months into the project. Two airports—Templehof and Gatow—were operating at peak capacity, but there was room for improvement at Tegel in the French sector. However, it was a low-use facility with runways unsuited to the ponderous weight of laden multi-engine aircraft. The obvious solution was to reinforce the runways or, better yet, build new ones. However, the large, heavy equipment required was unavailable in the area, and it was too cumbersome to be loaded aboard even the largest transport.

LeMay, harking back to the seemingly impossible construction performed by coolies at the China B-29 bases, felt that there must be a way. He put his staff to work and was presented with a unique concept: Cut the cement laying and paving machines into manageable pieces, fly them to Berlin, and weld them back together.

That solved half the problem. The other half concerned the immense amount of foundation material for a new runway—as deep as five feet in places. There simply was not enough airlift to deliver the required filler, so LeMay cast around and found the answer literally under his nose. Berlin had been bombed to rubble and not even the motivated, efficient Germans had been able to dispose of it. Consequently, the problem solved itself. Bricks and concrete chunks were trucked to Tegel, providing for the new runway while clearing the bombed-out city for renovation.

Vittles became a triumph of innovation, dedication, and inspiration. With their subordinates, LeMay, Smith, and Tunner wrote a new chapter in the history military airlift operations. In one sense they ran the most successful airline in history. During the fourteen months ending August 1949, Vittles logged 278,000 flights with 2.3 million tons of food, fuel, and supplies to Berlin's western sectors.

In comparison, the NATO effort to supply Sarajevo in 1992–1996 delivered 180,000 tons—a total exceeded in one month's airlift to Berlin.

But the astounding success came at a cost. By the time Vittles ended, twenty-eight air force fliers, three navy men, and thirty-nine British aircrew had died feeding Berlin. Weather-related accidents were by far the greatest cause of losses, especially in the dead of a northern European winter.

Late 1948 brought a season of change to the air force. Upon Carl Spaatz's retirement, Hoyt Vandenberg became chief of staff and he knew what he wanted to do. High on his list of priorities was shaking up the Strategic Air Command (SAC). Established in March 1946, SAC was one-third of the air force's combat structure with the Tactical Air Command and Air Defense Command. Under the often lackluster George C. Kenney, America's aerial deterrent force had little to show for more than two years of service.

Consequently, Hoyt Vandenberg sent out the word. The engineers were still leveling the new runway at Tegel when LeMay got orders stateside. He turned over command to Lieutenant General John K. Cannon, who was well experienced in Europe, having held the USAFE post in 1945–46. However, it is instructive that LeMay was still matching or exceeding general officers far senior to himself: Cannon was fourteen years older.

Back home, the Strategic Air Command represented a closely held secret: America had no significant nuclear strike force.

Curtis LeMay as a newly commissioned lieutenant in the Army
Air Corps, 1929. Despite his initial assignment to "pursuits,"
LeMay evolved into the service's leading heavy bomber advocate.
(USAF Museum)

The "double strike" on August 17, 1943 was the most ambitious mission
then flown by the Eighth Air Force. LeMay consults with Colonel Sullivan
and Joseph J. Preston of the 305th Group at Telergma, Algeria, after the
Regensburg shuttle mission to North Africa. (USAFA, Brown collection,
via Frederick A. Johnsen)

After leading the 305th Bomb Group for nearly a year LeMay held two commands as a brigadier general. This photo probably was taken in late 1943 when he led the Third Air Division. (USAF Museum)

Probably seen in 1945, the service stripes on LeMay's left sleeve indicate 2 ½ years of overseas duty. In fact, he spent about thirty-three months of World War II in Great Britain, China, and the Pacific combat theaters. (USAFA, Brown collection, via Frederick A. Johnsen)

In 1946 LeMay watched a radio-controlled B-17 directed by a ground controller in the Able and Baker nuclear tests at Bikini Atoll. (AFFTC/HO via Frederick A. Johnsen)

LeMay conferred with Brigadier General Haywood Hansell, previous commander of XXI Bomber Command, on Guam in early 1945. (AAFTC/HO via Fredrick A. Johnsen

Except on formal occasions, LeMay was seldom photographed without a pipe or cigar. Though he chewed stogies far more than he smoked them, he still nurtured the story that he once declared that a bomber "wouldn't dare" explode with the SAC commander puffing away beneath a wing. (USAF Museum)

Perhaps the toughest pose LeMay ever struck was aboard a U.S. Navy aircraft carrier. His opinion of the naval exercise he has just observed may be inferred by his expression—inscrutable. (USAF Museum)

On June 30, 1961, LeMay took the oath of office as Air Force Chief of Staff from Eugene Zuckert, Secretary of the Air Force. Onlookers included the two presidents whom LeMay would serve in that capacity: John F. Kennedy, and Lyndon B. Johnson, then vice president. (USAF Museum)

Nine rows of ribbons attest to LeMay's thirty-seven-year career, including a dozen combat decorations from the United States, Britain, Belgium, and the Soviet Union. (USAF Museum)

CHAPTER 7

SAC: Forging the Weapon

GENERAL CARL SPAATZ HAD ESTABLISHED THE STRATEGIC Air Command in March 1946 with the mission of conducting long-range offensive operations in any part of the world, using "the latest and most advanced weapons." The focus was almost wholly on the Soviet Union, clearly no longer a Western ally. Spaatz selected a colleague, General George C. Kenney, as SAC's first commander.

Kenney was an odd choice for SAC. A World War I veteran, he had made his name leading the Fifth Air Force in the Southwest Pacific 1942–45, and though popular with his men, he was an advocate of tactical aviation, possessing little experience with heavy bombers and none with B-29s. (The Fifth never had more than four Consolidated B-24 groups.) Additionally, Kenney had opposed B-29 operations from the Marianas, insisting that they would only harass the Japanese rather than harm them. While he may have been exhibiting a lack of vision, more likely he was concerned that Twentieth Air Force's move to the Pacific would divert logistics and materiel from his command.

Three years after VJ-Day, Kenney was seventeen years older than LeMay and clearly past his prime. Like most senior airmen, he was largely focused on winning the political battle for an independent air force. Consequently, he spent much time on the speaking circuit, leaving his command to fend for itself. A navy history of the era characterized SAC under Kenney as "two years of inadequate attention, skewed priorities, and outright command mismanagement."[1]

Organizationally, SAC controlled the Eighth and Fifteenth Air Forces; an impressive lineup on paper. In 1947 the command had sixteen very heavy bomb groups with B-29s and the larger B-50s. The next year, with a change in terminology, SAC grew to two very heavy (Convair B-36) groups and a dozen "medium" bomb groups with the older aircraft.

When LeMay assumed command in October 1948, SAC numbered some 50,000 personnel with an impressive sounding 837 aircraft, including over 200 piston fighters. But the offensive capability was nowhere near that potential: just thirty-five B-50s possessing intercontinental range and a similar number of new B-36s. Of LeMay's fourteen wings, none were at full strength. Only two flew the new B-50 version of the Superfortress; the others retained B-29s that lacked intercontinental range. In-flight refueling—essential to global operations—was in its infancy with merely two squadrons receiving KB-29 tankers.

Nor were the nuclear statistics any better. In late 1948 the United States had about 110 atomic bombs with nearly 60 nuclear-capable B-29, B-50, and B-36 aircraft in operational units. However, the atomic force was nowhere near fully operational, as there was little urgency in expanding the capability while America remained the world's only nuclear power.

In the period before the Soviets developed the ability to deliver nuclear weapons, LeMay believed that America could have reversed the postwar geography of Europe. In his view, it would have been possible to present Moscow with an ultimatum: withdraw from the occupied nations or face the destruction of the Soviet Union's warmaking ability. Furthermore, he felt that such an operation would have succeeded with no more losses than those involved in a comparable number of peacetime flying hours.

LeMay never presented his thoughts to President Truman or Eisenhower nor anyone else in the chain of command. He considered such options a policy matter to be decided by the civilian authorities, but never wavered in his certitude that the Russians would have backed down—as they did in Cuba—because they lacked the ability to retaliate in kind.

Later he wrote, "When you stand up and act like a man, you win respect. . . . It's when you fall back, shaking with apprehension, that you're apt to get into trouble."[2]

Meanwhile, he focused on building the Strategic Air Command.

SAC headquarters had been moved from Andrews Air Force Base near Washington, D.C., to Offutt Air Force Base near Omaha, Nebraska. The air force's choice of a heartland headquarters was instructive: It was beyond reach of Soviet attack, at least for the foreseeable future. However, when he arrived at Offutt, LeMay disappointed the civic reception committee, bluntly stating that SAC was nothing for Omaha or the air force to be proud of. And he intended to change that.

LeMay was appalled at what he found—and did not find. Not one bomb group was combat ready. Training had been neglected; few aircrew bothered with mission-oriented tasks such as high altitude flying or realistic navigation problems, let alone bombing, which was conducted on artificially enhanced radar reflectors.

For a mission-oriented commander like LeMay, Kenney's lack of attention to basics was unforgivable. SAC had no target lists and therefore no planned routes. Of equal concern, and for years thereafter, SAC did not even control its primary weapons. The Atomic Energy Committee retained authority over the stockpiled "nukes."

Kenney might have been forgiven some of his neglect, considering the high-stakes political game being played on Capitol Hill in the continuing service wars. But to most observers his deputy, Major General Clements McMullen, had been asleep at the throttle. Consequently, LeMay inherited a command deficient in everything that counted most: personnel, equipment, training—and morale.

Having spent time in the D.C. snake pit, LeMay thought better of expressing himself so forthrightly in Washington as he had in Omaha. At a dinner party in November, Defense Secretary James Forrestal asked SAC's new commander in chief (CinC) about prospects for attacking strategic targets inside Russia. LeMay hedged his bets by stating that SAC could accomplish its mission with minimal losses, assuming that an offensive involving 80 percent of the nuclear inventory was launched early enough. At the time, that was of course an unwarranted assumption, given the command's poor readiness. Another guest, Rear Admiral William S. Parsons, the weaponeer over Hiroshima, was familiar with SAC's lamentable condition, but declined to contradict LeMay, recognizing that the air force man had just fallen heir to a fragile fiefdom.[3]

LeMay realized that he would have to build SAC from the ground up.

Offutt had been the B-29 factory in which the *Enola Gay* was built. Once bustling with activity, in 1948 it was a largely abandoned facility with "a cockeyed runway" and not much else. LeMay established his command's new headquarters in the old Martin Aircraft facility that he found guarded by a sergeant armed with a ham sandwich. Existing housing was substandard, including tarpaper barracks. That unhappy fact precipitated a battle to get decent quarters for his people.

LeMay's vision of SAC was formed early on, based on a twenty-four-hour wartime readiness. Under those circumstances, barracks living was unworkable. Few men could get enough sleep with others coming off duty at all hours, playing cards, listening to the radio, or just kibitzing. LeMay established a standard arrangement: two-man rooms with adjoining baths between rooms. The atmosphere became quiet, efficient, restful.

When time and resources permitted, he began building on-base housing for married personnel. For a time in the 1950s he even wrangled a series of four and one-half year mortgages.

While no epicure, LeMay had long experience of military food. He knew the relationship between chow and morale, and found new ways of improving air force fare. He sent Offutt's base cooks to the better restaurants in Omaha, learning to prepare more appetizing dishes for the base facilities. Some union bosses complained, fearing that the military "scabs" would harm the employment prospects for union members. But LeMay countered with the ob servation that the military cooks were not taking civilian jobs—the understudies were still paid by the government and soon returned to the base.

Recreational activities included hobby shops, custom car garages, ham radio stations, even aero clubs where nonpilots could learn to fly civilian aircraft. During his SAC tenure LeMay built two hotrods himself and supervised fitting a jet engine to a race car chassis. Nothing would do but for the commander in chief to perform "test pilot" duties, resulting in a vehicle that went extremely fast but was difficult to stop. LeMay solved the problem by installing a drag chute.

With improved quarters, food, and morale, the reenlistment rate climbed five points from 1954 to 1955. The results of LeMay's "people programs" showed not only in greater efficiency, but in greater retention.

Despite his initial anger at SAC's poor condition, LeMay decided to give his fledgling command a chance to prove itself. In January 1949, two months after his optimistic statements to Forrestal, he laid on a SAC-wide practice mission against Wright-Patterson Air Force Base Ohio. The problem was complicated by thunderstorms over Ohio, which forced crews to fly at unaccustomed high altitudes. In the end, not one bomber completed the mission. The service was so embarrassed that the summary was still classified six-teen years later. Not even LeMay could obtain a copy.[4]

In order to effect a positive change, LeMay reached into his professional talent pool and began pulling out names of men he knew and trusted. He retrieved Thomas Power from impending attaché duty in England and made him deputy commander. John B. Montgomery, erstwhile XXI Bomber Command operations officer, was handed SAC operations, and Walter "Cam" Sweeney, another Marianas alumnus, took over plans. Augie Kissner, an Eighth Air Force associate, was fetched from Germany to become chief of staff.

LeMay tapped another of his UK veterans, Colonel Russell E. Schleeh, as his aide. By then Schleeh was known as the air force's chief bomber test pilot who had flown the futuristic Northrop XB-49 Flying Wing. Extraordinarily versatile, he also won the national hydroplane championship.

LeMay's team began building SAC one group at a time, starting with the 509th, Paul Tibbets's old outfit that had destroyed Hiroshima and Nagasaki. Now at Roswell, New Mexico, the one nuclear-capable group was led by Bill Irvine, LeMay's innovative, energetic supply officer on Guam. LeMay considered the 509th the best of a bad lot, and in January 1950 he gave Irvine the considerable responsibility of getting the new Convair B-36 up and running. Recently promoted to brigadier, Irvine got with the program and made LeMay's six-month deadline for combat capability with the huge, long-ranged bomber.

The B-36 had arrived in SAC almost the same day as LeMay. The prototype had flown in August 1946 with initial deliveries in June 1948. During a twelve-year production run, Convair delivered 382 Peacemakers, despite complaints from clergy that the bomber's name constituted heresy.

The '36 was huge, an aerial leviathan that dwarfed anything else. It spanned 230 feet (90 more than a B-29) and its empty weight was twice that of a Superfortress. With 21,000 gallons on board, the Peacemaker's fuel weighed nearly as much as a combat-loaded B-29. Fully loaded, the Peacemaker was capable of a 7,000-mile range, giving SAC a genuine intercontinental capability.

For LeMay, the B-36 represented yet another challenge: incorporating an extremely sophisticated weapon into his growing arsenal while building the force's infrastructure, personnel, and operating procedures. His leadership perspective was generally focused on the future as much as the present, and apart from equipment, that meant finding larger numbers of more qualified people.

To man his new units, LeMay's search extended to the air force's bitter rival, the U.S. Navy. A keen judge of talent, he recruited some outstanding naval aviators with promises of rapid advancement and greater responsibility in SAC. His star acquisition was Lieutenant Commander Patrick D. Fleming, the Navy's fourth-ranking ace and an accomplished test pilot. Within a month of transferring to the air force, he was promoted to lieutenant colonel, a grade ahead of his naval contemporaries. LeMay tapped him for the jet bomber project in 1950, but Colonel Fleming died in the first B-52 loss six years later.

When he took over SAC, LeMay thought that even with the command's weak structure, it could have defeated the Soviet Union with nuclear weapons. SAC's first war plan was drafted in 1949, and it was vintage LeMay. He proposed delivering the entire nuclear arsenal: 133 weapons against seventy Russian cities in a month-long deluge. His concept of overwhelming force, so dramatically proven in Japan, was to be applied on an even greater scale against the Soviet Union.[5]

As to the question of how much deterrence was enough, LeMay felt there could never be too much—only too little. At the core of deterrence, of course, was the enemy's perception of one's willingness and ability to retaliate—or to strike first in event of provocation.

The challenge for current airpower theorists and operators is no different than LeMay faced. Deterrence remains a doctrinal mission for the U.S. Air Force, and whatever the technical progress since the

1940s, the objective remains identical: deterring potential aggressors in preference to fighting them. LeMay understood and accepted the fact that politicians determine national goals and strategy, but he knew that without a credible force, the loftiest goals inevitably would fail. Consequently, he saw an improved SAC not only as an aim unto itself, but as a crucial national goal, especially in context of thermonuclear weapons and the cold war.

LeMay and SAC planners realized that as the Soviets increased their nuclear capability, U.S. targeting would necessarily move from industrial centers of production to enemy offensive systems, mainly bombers and missiles. Thus was born the "counterforce" theory of targeting, a concept that LeMay grasped and advocated.

The debate occurred at a time when nuclear strategy was still evolving. Some theorists believed that a phased bombing campaign could be effective in demonstrating American-Western resolve while limiting the destruction and collateral damage inside the Soviet Union and Warsaw Pact countries. In that respect, it was an eerily attractive option: If there were going to be a nuclear war, presumably it could be limited to Russian military bases.

Gradualism was anathema to LeMay's professional instincts. He advocated a massive strike—by preemption if necessary—that would leave much of the Soviet Union a pile of radioactive rubble. And he had enormous faith in his command's ability to deliver on his concept, eventually with a "restrike" plan that in some places would "bounce the rubble" left by the first attack. The phrase that was popularized in the 1960s was "overkill"—the assurance that a crucial target received two or more weapons.

Today, "overkill" is seldom addressed, and rarely if ever in a nuclear context. In the post–cold war era, military leaders are far less concerned with nuclear targeting than with what the media may perceive as excessive use of conventional weapons. Given the capabilities of 1950s ordnance, LeMay would not have bothered himself with such things. His experience involved massive use of high explosives and incendiaries against large targets (urban industrial areas) in contrast to today's pinpoint attacks with precision-guided munitions. When atomic bombs became available, he transferred the existing doctrine to the next step in technical-scientific progress, yielding similar results for vastly less effort. Hiroshima and Nagasaki were destroyed by single B-29s whereas hundreds were required for comparable destruction before. In the thermonuclear era, overkill became a question of two versus three bombs on a target. In the era of global terrorism, one 750-pounder may be regarded as "overkill," depending on what it hits.

In response to the first Russian nuclear test, in January 1950 President Truman called for bigger bombs with a thermonuclear (fusion) capability. The next summer American scientists induced a 225-kiloton explosion at Eniwetok Atoll in the Pacific, but the first practical fusion bomb test occurred almost eighteen months later. In October 1952 the "Mike shot" produced over ten megatons of explosive power, leading the way to greater nuclear potential.

<hr/>

When he took over SAC in 1948, LeMay had twenty years of experience with the military. He knew that institutional knowledge was a fragile commodity, having seen various entities reinvent the wheel time and again. Consequently, he fell back on a time-tested means of establishing a corporate memory in the form of manuals.

Certainly military manuals were nothing new; they had been around almost as long as the printing press. But sometimes they were ignored, often because of obsolescence. Therefore, LeMay not only had manuals written for every job in the command, from combat crews to motor pool managers, but he appointed officers to keep them current. Standardization was the byword: Failure to follow established procedures was likely to land a base or wing commander on Curt LeMay's carpet.

A big part of LeMay's standardization program was rigid adherence to checklists. As an accomplished, methodical pilot, he knew the tendency of many senior airmen to become complacent after years in the cockpit. He saw a pattern: high-time pilots involved in a disproportionate number of accidents. He initiated a relentless campaign for following established procedures and got remarkable results. When he took over, the accident rate was an appalling sixty-five per hundred thousand flying hours. When he left, it was three, and that was not wholly satisfactory to him.

LeMay also knew that repetition was the heart of competence: not merely going through the motions but executing each task thoroughly and properly. He had his crews fly thousands of practice missions within the United States. Every city over 25,000 population was "bombed" repeatedly in practice missions; San Francisco alone was "attacked" 600 times in one month. Eventually SAC crews could perform their complex, demanding tasks to LeMay's high standards on a routine basis.

Yet there was far more to standardization than established procedures or even an integrated doctrine. LeMay's leadership philosophy also fell under his definition of standardization, meaning consistent goals. His three pillars of leadership were:

> People needed to believe in their work; a product of inspirational leadership and self motivation.
>
> People needed to see visible progress toward the organization's stated goal, no matter how incremental the improvement.
>
> People needed recognition and appreciation for their contributions toward the goal.[6]

LeMay frequently used his personal experience to improve SAC. He recalled that at Langley before the war he had made himself "triple rated" as a pilot, navigator, and bombardier, largely before the concept was even identified. Consequently, he formulated a policy of cross training many officers and aircrew in two or more roles: pilots and bombardiers who could navigate, and navigators who could bomb. Some pilots considered themselves a cut above "mere" crew until the commanding general made it plain that pilots existed for one purpose: to put bombardiers in position to destroy a target. That was not possible without expert navigation over perhaps thousands of miles.

There was more. In England LeMay had helped instigate the lead crew concept, and continued that successful procedure in both B-29 commands. Consequently, a new lead crew school was formed at Walters Air Force Base, Texas, composed of "R" designated crews who were already rated combat ready. The coveted "E" designation was applied only to lead crews while the ultimate was "S" status, making the crew eligible for spot promotions.

The spot promotion was one of LeMay's most effective methods of enhancing efficiency and building morale. At the end of 1949, barely a year after assuming command, he gained approval of the air force personnel director to grant immediate promotions to junior officers who excelled in their duties. Originally the concept only applied to first lieutenants flying as aircraft commanders, but over the next two years it was expanded to all aircrew. However, the promotions were temporary until sufficient time had passed in the new grade to justify making them permanent. Those airmen who failed to maintain the standards found their promotions revoked.

There were various ways to earn a spot promotion. One of the best bets was to win or place well up in the annual SAC bombing competition. But the crews or individuals who handled an emergency especially well or devised an innovative procedure also could gain LeMay's praise.

LeMay established the practice of assembling "flyaway kits" with essential spare parts and equipment to support aircraft and crews thousands of miles from home. The variety was enormous: the larger kits contained 44,000 items. He arranged for his units to deploy overseas on a rotational basis, learning first hand the local operating environment and base facilities. It was an extension of the

1943 lead crew concept, but expanding that specialist basis to the entire command.

Almost within hours of Japan's surrender, the Army Air Forces and the U.S. Navy began a prolonged, bitter battle against their devoted enemies: each other. At the center of the feud was whether air force bombers or navy aircraft carriers were best suited to defending the nation. It culminated in what was called "the revolt of the admirals."

In August 1949 the House Armed Services Committee began its "B-36 hearings," examining capabilities of the controversial new bomber versus the navy's aircraft carriers. The navy, sensitive to charges that it could not deliver nuclear weapons from the sea, had rushed into production a minimal offensive capability with the North American AJ-1 Savage. However, given the administration's bitter antinaval bias, the admirals recognized any political threat as potentially lethal.

As Commander in Chief of Strategic Air Command, (CinC-SAC), LeMay was unavoidably called to testify before Congress during the hearing. He thoroughly detested the obligation, being personally averse to politics and professionally disgusted at the command's poor condition. Some of his air force colleagues had not endeared themselves to the politicians holding the purse strings: Kenney for instance had responded to inquiries about Soviet guided missiles by discussing night fighters. Clearly he was being evasive under close questioning.

Furthermore, Kenney had conceded that the original B-36 had sustained a long, painful gestation period, which in truth was to be expected of so revolutionary a design. Previously, however, he had expressed doubt as to its viability as a strategic weapon. Once the navy–air force battle heated up, he adjusted his testimony, contending that the Peacemaker had since been upgraded and should be able to perform its mission, though probably not in daytime.[7]

Following Kenney's potentially damning testimony, LeMay was asked about operating the new bomber only at night. He replied in no uncertain terms, insisting that SAC crews could operate the new bomber day or night, singly or in groups, in any weather. Under further questioning about the Russian defenses, he stated that by flying above the radar coverage, and thus avoiding interception, B-36s could attack undetected until their bombs exploded on target.[8]

LeMay's assertions, probably honestly held, may not have reflected SAC's full capability at that time. He had been in command for nearly a year and was making progress toward redressing the situation he inherited from Kenney. But many of his bomb wings were not up to his standards that summer, and it is likely that LeMay was speaking of a best-case scenario for some—certainly not all—of his units.

Meanwhile, additional pro-bomber claims continued emanating from other representatives. Secretary of the Air Force Stuart Symington alluded to the B-36's heavy battery of defensive weapons: as many as sixteen 20mm cannon. However, he omitted any mention that the Peacemaker's fire control system was largely inoperable.

Doctrine held that the "penetrating bomber" (that is, the B-36) could avoid the teeth of Soviet defenses to reach any target in range. However, the navy cited an Eglin Field report in 1948 citing fighter interceptions of Peacemakers flying at 40,000 feet. LeMay was specifically asked about Russian radar capability and responded that an aircraft flying high enough could probably avoid detection. Later, when General Hoyt Vandenberg was questioned about the validity of that assessment, he could not provide a positive answer. Though both officers may have been disingenuous, it is equally possible that the capability of Soviet radars was unknown at the time.[9]

Much of the "dark blue–light blue" acrimony was swept away in a contaminated wind that September of 1949. The Soviets had detonated their first atomic device, with radioactive elements detected by U.S. reconnaissance aircraft. The threat of atomic attack on the American mainland loomed hugely in Washington, though professionals recognized that Russian weapon production was bound to remain small for the near term, and the ability to deliver such weapons also was limited.

Nonetheless, the arms race soon escalated. By the end of 1950 the U.S. nuclear inventory was up to 350 warheads; Russia had about five. Five years later the U.S. arsenal contained some 3,000 warheads; Russia 200. In 1959 the Soviet total passed 1,000.[10]

Faced with a Soviet nuclear capability, LeMay and SAC had to adapt to a changing world. The original war plan, largely aimed at Russian industry, turned increasingly toward Soviet bomber bases and aircraft factories. With more targets, SAC required the ability to deliver more bombs, which in turn drove the number of bombers, crews, and bases.

Whatever the warhead count, more than ever, SAC needed intelligence. Reconnaissance flights, defectors, and covert methods all contributed to the growing list of target files, but SAC seldom had as much information as it preferred.

Once again, LeMay's circle of friends and colleagues provided the help he needed. LeMay's former classmate Frank Armstrong had become chief of the Alaskan Air Command (AAC), the one American unit on the periphery of the Soviet Union. Facing the Russian bear across the frigid Bering Sea, AAC's reconnaissance aircraft were well within reach of Soviet bases in Siberia. Therefore, Armstrong equipped RB-29s with the most powerful cameras available—some with Harvard-designed 100-inch focal lengths—and sent them snooping along the icy periphery of the nascent Evil Empire.

In 1949, not long after LeMay took over SAC, Armstrong contended that any offensive plans originating in Siberia would become evident in the stockpiling of supplies to support a logistics base. As chief of the overall Alaskan command, General Nathan F. Twining concurred, noting that the dearth of highways and minimal rail lines in the area would force the Russians to build up their forces by sea. Alaskan Air Command easily could monitor sea borne traffic.

However, the thirty-mile observation capability of the RB-29s was negated almost at the start. The Truman administration, fearful of antagonizing the Soviets, prohibited recon flights closer than forty miles offshore.

The restrictions ended that September when the Soviet nuclear detonation was discovered.

America needed new aircraft for a new postwar world, and they arrived in a mind-numbing succession of types and numbers inconceivable today. But not only new designs appeared on the flight line: equally important, so did new capabilities.

In September 1950 two Republic F-84E fighters took off from RAF Manston and headed west. The mission was led by Colonel David C. Schilling—one of LeMay's favorite fighter pilots—who two years previously had led the first mass transatlantic crossing with four en route fuel stops. His wingman, experiencing engine trouble, had to eject near Goose Bay, Newfoundland, while Schilling completed the 3,300 miles to Limestone, Maine, in barely ten hours. The Americans were refueled in flight by British tankers, an indication of greater cooperation between the allies.

For the air force, Schilling's success was a public relations bonus. For LeMay, it was further confirmation that his strategic escort wings could deploy with the bombers in time of crisis. Before long, transoceanic crossings by jet fighters became routine evolutions.

In his first four years at SAC, LeMay relied upon older aircraft for the bulk of his offensive airpower. The B-29 was his most numerous bomber through 1952, with the follow-on B-50 remaining in declining numbers until 1955. But LeMay kept an eye on the horizon, building toward an all-jet force with truly global reach.

If SAC were going to meet its mission of projecting airpower around the globe, the bombers needed more range. That meant in-flight refueling, which no less a figure than Tooey Spaatz had pioneered for the Air Corps in 1929.

The air force demonstrated a genuine in-flight refueling capability with a round-the-world record in March 1949. A B-50 made the first nonstop circumnavigation in ninety-four hours, refueled en route by four KB-29s. The previous air force record, achieved by two B-29s, took fifteen days.

Ironically, for awhile neither LeMay nor his requirements staffer, Jack J. Catton, believed that tanker operations would become routine. The conventional wisdom held that specialized equipment and techniques would limit the option to specific missions. Meanwhile, the B-36 was the only bomber with intercontinental range on internal fuel.

Despite his early misgivings about tankers, LeMay proved adaptable to changing requirements. The main impetus for tankers—and before long, jet tankers—was the next-generation bomber, the elegant Boeing B-47.

Looking more like a large fighter than a bomber, the B-47 Stratojet was fast, capable, and "produceable" with more than 2,000 built. It first flew in December 1947 with initial deliveries three years later, but combat radius was less than 2,000 miles. Consequently, when the early wings stood up in 1951, LeMay had to deploy his B-47s beyond the continental United States, to Alaska, Britain, Morocco, and Spain in order to reach targets in the Soviet Union.

However, SAC turned a corner in 1953 when B-47 production allowed 329 Stratojets in the inventory at year's end. That was a significant figure: 43 percent of LeMay's bombers, with the B-36 exceeding both the B-29 and B-50.

For all his love of flying, LeMay was seldom if ever sentimental about airplanes. However, he was extremely concerned about his aircrews, and on their behalf he established what amounted to a global rescue service.

Early in SAC's career, when in-flight refueling was limited, LeMay realized that in a war with Russia he stood to lose many of his crews, especially from the relatively short-ranged B-47s. Therefore, Colonel Demitrius Stampedos made a bold suggestion: Establish a unit dedicated to retrieving downed bomber crews from the Soviet Union. The risks were obvious, but as a rescue pilot said,

"Curt cared about his people." Therefore, in August 1950, the Eighth Air Rescue Squadron (ARS) was activated at Camp Carson, near Colorado Springs.[11]

Stampedos and LeMay selected a barren region in Russia as a huge "rendezvous" area. Bomber crews lacking fuel to reach friendly territory were briefed to fly to the area and eject with fifteen minutes of fuel remaining. The pilotless bombers would continue to their destruction far from the rescue areas. Once three crews were assembled, they would use secure radios to arrange a pickup.

Enter the Eighth Air Rescue Squadron. Each Douglas C-47's five-man crew had a special waiver to ignore air force regulations regarding weather and altitude. (At least one pilot logged more than 2,000 hours below 100 feet altitude—normally against regulations—but never had to use his "get out of jail free card" with LeMay's private phone number.)

During the squadron's first operational inspection, LeMay arrived with manufacturer Donald Douglas, who watched the Eighth operate from a 1,200-foot dirt strip, flying at fifty feet maximum in daylight and one hundred feet at night. At the end of the trial Douglas said, "I have watched you for three days, and gentlemen, the C-47 can't do what you have just done."[12]

Perhaps one measure of the squadron's importance was the assignment of its well regarded maintenance officer, Lieutenant Colonel Lloyd LeMay, the CinC's younger brother. However, insiders noted that, whether from sibling issues or concern over propriety, Curt and Lloyd seldom spoke, other than in the line of duty.

The Eighth ARS practiced constantly, learning the best way of entering hostile skies in preparation for "the real thing." The squadron became so proficient that in its first two and a half years, its C-47s penetrated North American airspace 130 times with only one interception, when a plane had to pop up to avoid cloud-shrouded mountains. The C-47s were equally successful operating in NATO airspace.

One of the notable ARS pilots was a World War II ace, Major William H. Allen. He said, "Curt loved his people. He could get new airplanes quick, but he couldn't get qualified people quick."[13]

Meanwhile, after 1951 the new B-47 acquired longer legs and the B-52 was inbound in 1955 so the "taxi service" was transferred to Military Airlift Command in September 1954.

Hand in glove with the B-47 Stratojet was the KC-135 Stratotanker, one of the most successful military aircraft of all time. Boeing had produced nearly 600 piston-powered KC-97s but the advantages of a jet tanker were obvious: compatible performance with jet bombers. Therefore, the company developed the KC-135 from its 707 airliner, delivering the tanker version to SAC in an astonishing ten months of 1956–57. With advent of the Stratotanker, LeMay's vision approached fruition: He had conceived a unified all-jet force and convinced Congress to fund it. Today, the Stratotanker remains one of his enduring legacies, likely to remain in service until 2020.

LeMay believed in communicating with the troops, and in 1950 he inaugurated *Professional Pilot,* the SAC publication. By year's end it had been renamed *Combat Crew,* another step toward the professionalism he sought throughout the command, stressing flying safety as the means to optimum readiness. In the first issue he wrote, "As long as airplanes are flown by human beings we are going to have accidents. Some accidents will be unavoidable. However, by doing everything possible to reduce those caused through human errors, we can keep our accidents down to the minimum. . . . The goal of the publication will be to help you perform your job in a professional matter. Only a professional performance on your part will provide maximum safety for yourself and your crew."[14]

The magazine remained in print for forty-two years, until the month before SAC was dissolved in 1992.

LeMay recognized that SAC would have to prove itself, especially given its lackluster early record. Some things he could affect immediately—procedures, training, and commanders—but others would require time and money. Despite his aversion to the Washington political game, he became an adept player, establishing allies if not friends and indulging in what a later generation would call "networking." It was a multifront war, waged within the air force, Defense Department, Congress, and the Bureau of the Budget.

During his time as CinCSAC, LeMay established close ties with Washington's most influential men. Most prominent were two Georgia Democrats: Senator Richard B. Russell, who had been elected in 1932, and Democrat Representative Carl Vinson, whose tenure dated from 1914. Both were chairmen of their respective armed forces committees.

As chairman of the House Armed Services Committee Vinson said, "The most expensive thing in the world is a cheap army and navy." The same applied to the air force. Though partial to the navy, Vinson was especially air-minded. While he personally disliked flying, he supported establishment of the army air corps and eventually an independent air force. LeMay ensured that SAC maintained cordial relations with Mr. Vinson.

<hr/>

When North Korea invaded the South on June 25, 1950, SAC was still building. Nine days after the war began, General Hoyt Vandenberg ordered two SAC groups to Japan, where the B-29s presumably could interrupt Communist logistics. LeMay's former counterpart, Lieutenant General Rosey O'Donnell, then commanding the Fifteenth Air Force, ran the operation. When the first two groups returned to the continental United States, two more were deployed to the Far East for the duration of the war.

LeMay was not pleased with the situation. He sent his least-prepared units rather than detract from SAC's nuclear mission, which he regarded as paramount. When politically inspired limits were imposed (lest China be provoked) LeMay saw the writing on the bulkhead. He concluded that his bombers never did hit a strategic target—the only kind he considered worthwhile.[9]

However, SAC did provide a nuclear option as a contingency. General Power, the "X-Ray" (Far East) air commander in Tokyo, had the Forty-third Bomb Wing at Guam with a strategic capability in case the theater commanders—Generals Douglas MacArthur and later Matthew Ridgway—decided to play that card. LeMay calculated that the X-Ray B-50s could deliver a nuclear strike on sixteen hours notice. It was a vast improvement on the peacetime arrangement of five days to plan, load, and launch a nuclear mission.

LeMay found himself in a position of ambivalence. While he favored the option of using atomic weapons if necessary, he did not approve of the warning order received from the Joint Chiefs in July. They directed ten aircraft and qualified crews to deliver atomic bombs (minus the nuclear components) to Guam, ready for use in Korea. LeMay and SAC generally were opposed to the idea on principle: It looked like further dissipation of rare strategic assets to field commanders.

In short order, LeMay as CinCSAC and Vandenberg as air force chief of staff reached a consensus: the bombs and aircraft would proceed as ordered, but under JCS (Joint Chiefs of Staff) control rather than MacArthur's. Since SAC reported to the joint chiefs, LeMay retained de facto control.

On August 5, 1950, ten B-29s departed Fairfield-Suisun Air Force Base, California, each carrying an unarmed weapon. But one Superfortress crashed on takeoff. The impact and subsequent detonation of the weapon's explosive trigger killed nineteen people aboard the bomber and on the ground, including the mission commander, Brigadier General Robert F. Travis, yet another of LeMay's dwindling circle of flight school classmates.

Despite the planning for an atomic strike, neither LeMay, the air force, nor even the Defense Department controlled the weapons, as America's nuclear arsenal was owned by the Atomic Energy Commission. LeMay recalled, "Those bombs were too horrible and too dangerous to entrust to the military. . . . Our troops guarded them but we didn't own them."[16]

SAC did, however, manage to retain the remaining nine bombs. Partly as a result of the Travis incident, the air force gained control of its nuclear weapons in 1951, a logical arrangement given the short response time in event of a strategic exchange with the Soviets.

SAC regarded the Korean War as a frustrating experience. LeMay and his acolytes saw a quick way to end North Korean aggression: man up and launch against Manchuria, burn down the principal cities, and deprive the aggressors of the malevolent factories supporting aggression in South Korea. That was the view from Omaha; the Washington perspective was more complex. The trouble was, Manchuria lay north of the Yalu River, in the People's Republic of China, which Harry S. Truman devoutly wished to avoid provoking. It was a foolish concern since at least a quarter million Chinese troops swarmed south at the end of 1950. But there were pragmatic concerns as well. Manchuria produced relatively little equipment for the Communist ground forces, and the Soviets provided the high-tech equipment: jet aircraft, radars, and the like.

Nobody advocated nuking Russia to save South Korea.

LeMay had one unit in the Far East when war broke out in June 1950, the 19th Bomb Wing. Requests for reinforcements prompted him to deploy the Twenty-second Wing from California and the Ninety-second from Washington state. They were selected for overseas service because they were largely lacking nuclear capability.

However, the hard-pressed allied forces in-theater wanted more and more airpower, especially since tactical units had all but abandoned the peninsula in the face of overwhelming enemy numbers. Faced with a request for two more bomb wings to support Korea, LeMay expressed concern about "too many splinters whittled off the stick." Nevertheless, he complied and sent the Ninety-Eighth, again from Spokane, Washington, and the 307th from Florida.[17]

Disappointed as he was at dilution of his carefully hoarded strike force, LeMay was far too professional to tolerate halfway measures. He wanted his B-29s employed as effectively as possible and dispatched Rosey O'Donnell to head bomber command in Japan. The irony could hardly have been missed: Five years previously O'Donnell had been instrumental in razing Japanese cities; now he commanded another B-29 force operating from the home islands.

Despite O'Donnell's presence, the "medium" bombers were largely employed in tactical operations. Neither he nor LeMay were remotely pleased when the Superforts were continually targeted against enemy forces and logistics rather than strategic points—which lay out of political reach across the Yalu. Nevertheless, the bombers could hit bridges and enemy positions south of the river, as well as the occasional airfield still operable in the north. But in 1951 the B-29s were driven from daytime skies. Swift MiG-15s, flown by experienced Russian pilots, inflicted unsustainable losses on the Boeings, despite squadrons of F-84 and F-86 fighter escorts.

When the B-47 went operational in 1951 its speed and altitude performance attracted the attention of the Far East command. Stratojets were capable of outpacing the MiG-15, and the RB-47 variants could safely overfly Communist territory to gain imagery and electronic intelligence. It seemed a logical request.

LeMay flatly refused.

Having finally gained jet bombers and recon aircraft, LeMay was adamant that they not be dispersed in peripheral chores that diluted his primary mission: strategic deterrence. Beyond that, teething troubles with the new design kept it only marginally operational until 1953. Consequently, the Superfortresses continued flying over Korea.

In the end, South Korea was largely saved by airpower but not by B-29s. Communist logistics were prevented from accumulating enough supplies to sustain a drive south of the prewar border, the thirty-eighth parallel, thanks to tactical aircraft of the air force, U.S. naval services, and allies.

Amid the urgent concerns of the Korean War, LeMay made history on October 29, 1951, when he received his fourth star at age forty-four. Thus, he became the youngest full general since Ulysses S. Grant eighty-five years before. LeMay's selection for the signal honor represented a confluence of events and requirements, not least of which was aviation itself. America's first military pilots only dated from 1909, when LeMay was three. He had literally grown up with airpower, and the newly independent air force required young leaders. None were younger than forty-four-year-old Curt LeMay.

By comparison, Hoyt Vandenberg pinned on his fourth star at age forty-nine in 1947. Arnold, Spaatz, and Kenney had been in their mid- to late fifties while LeMay's predecessors as chief of staff—Nathan Twining and Thomas D. White—were fifty-three and fifty-one, respectively.

One of the least-told stories of the Korean War was the means by which the armistice was achieved. President Dwight Eisenhower, newly elected and pledged to end the fighting, let it be known via Indian diplomats that he would authorize nuclear strikes if a settlement were not forthcoming. However, the nuclear capable B-29s would be subject to sabotage in South Korea, and could not be based on Okinawa or Japan for diplomatic reasons. Consequently, the Atlantic Fleet aircraft carrier USS *Lake Champlain* was deployed with a nuclear qualified air group. "The Champ" arrived off Korea in June 1953, operating Douglas AD Skyraiders and McDonnell F2H Banshees, both able to deliver atomic bombs. The message was received in Beijing.

LeMay became heartsick when Truman's no-win policy was sustained by President Eisenhower. The 1953 armistice seemed an appalling concession of vastly superior American military power: accepting a tie when LeMay believed a win was possible.

LeMay believed that Korea was bound to remain an exception to the concept of unlimited war. However, barely a decade later, America repeated the process in Vietnam, attempting to conduct an Asian land war with limited goals: the kind of folly that Curtis LeMay simply could not envision.

At the end of 1953 LeMay commanded seventeen wings of which eleven were actually equipped. B-47 strength had mushroomed from 62 to 329 Stratojets while B-36s remained significant: 185 bombers and 137 recon aircraft. By then the B-29 was on its way out, finally outnumbered both by B-36s and B-47s. Additionally, the command disposed of 502 tankers and 235 fighters. But more was on the way.

If any image represented the cold war, it was the Boeing B-52 Stratofortress. Its status became iconic: No other aircraft so thoroughly defined the era. Similarly, other than the B-29, it is also the aircraft most closely identified with Curtis LeMay.

The Stratofortress began life immediately after World War II when the army air forces requested proposals for an intercontinental bomber. The Convair B-36 was already contracted, but revolutionary advances in aviation clearly meant that the Peacemaker would be surpassed.

The B-52 became operational at Castle Air Force Base in June 1955, becoming the backbone of SAC from there on. Nearly 750 were built through 1962.

Not everyone was completely sold on the B-52. It was large, relatively complex, and would require additional funding for suitable hangars, hardstands, and runways. LeMay conceded all those points but insisted that the Stratofortress was worth the effort. In its capacious airframe he saw room to grow—"stretch" for new systems— and he believed the extra infrastructure would prove useful well downstream. He was proven right.

Air Force Secretary Donald Quarles (1955–59) called the '52 "The most formidable expression of air power in the history of military aviation."[18] LeMay would not have disagreed, though he remained notably unsentimental toward specific aircraft during his three decades in uniform. However, Boeing built everything significant to him during that period: from the B-17 to the B-29, B-47, B-52, and KC-135.

LeMay's assessment of the B-52 placed it far ahead of its predecessors. The B model cruised faster than the B-47 and more than twice as fast as the B-36, slightly exceeding the Peacemaker's combat radius and easily outdistancing the '47. With in-flight refueling the B-52 achieved unlimited range—a true intercontinental bomber—with a six-man crew to share the workload of the B-47's three men. LeMay finally had the weapon he felt that he needed.

LeMay believed in deterrence but he did not advocate absorbing the first strike—especially in a nuclear war. He believed that America's stated policy against launching the first blow was pragmatically and ethically absurd: It seemed to invite the Soviets to attempt a knockout in the opening seconds of the first round. In his 1968 treatise, *America Is in Danger*, he wrote, "Deterrence cannot be achieved with a second strike façade. It must rest not on the ability to withstand a first strike and retaliate effectively, but on the ability to launch a first strike and win if necessary." He cited the Cuban missile crisis as a case in point: Moscow was heavily outgunned in the atomic arena, and backed down.[19]

Preemptive attack has a long history in warfare: In the twentieth century alone it accounted for events as diverse as Pearl Harbor in 1941 and the Arab-Israeli War of 1967. LeMay had to deal with the possibility of launching or receiving a first strike, especially since a Soviet nuclear attack would deprive him of a major portion of his command. However, he built a force structure calculated to survive with sufficient strength to destroy most of the enemy's resources.

Certain similarities exist for twenty-first century commanders, particularly regarding Iraq. While Saddam Hussein's ability to produce nuclear bombs was not a genuine concern after 1991, the perception that he could employ chemical or biological weapons spurred the American invasion in 2003. Because he had used gas against Iran in the 1980s and against his own population thereafter, Saddam's actions triggered a preemptive attack by the Western coalition to prevent a repetition.

The difference between LeMay's very real cold war concerns and the Bush administration's perception of Saddam's intentions is primarily one of scale. A Soviet preemptive strike against America would have been devastating at best; apocalyptic at worst. Conversely, Iraq never possessed the ability to inflict even a small percentage of Russia's destruction upon America or the West, but in the wake of the 2001 terrorist attacks, preemption became a viable option. (Arguments as to the wisdom of leaving Saddam in power after 1991 will continue indefinitely, but the post–Desert Storm situation merits study in context of preemptive doctrine.)

In any case, as he advocated during the Cuban crisis and in Vietnam, LeMay favored massive application of force both in response to aggression, and in preemption. "Fighting on the cheap" made no sense to him, ethically, doctrinally, strategically, or tactically.

Ironically, much of the cold war vocabulary revolved around a few terms that the practitioners seldom subscribed to, nor even agreed upon, including "graduated response," "massive retaliation," and "mutually assured destruction". Geopolitical doves were fond of noting the latter's acronym, citing "MAD" as proof of the insanity they perceived in the nuclear arms race. In the end, of course, the MADness proved wholly successful with end of the Soviet Union and SAC's stand down in 1992.

Probably the testiest response from nuclear warriors was elicited by "massive retaliation." In 1984 several former SAC generals discussed the era with air force historians, assessing the philosophy and conduct of strategic deterrence. LeMay was asked if in the 1950s "massive retaliation" was seen as a general nuclear war. He thought that the phrase was coined by a journalist or public affairs officer, and explained his definition:

> Too many people thought of massive retaliation as pushing all the buttons . . . in response to virtually anything the Russians did. Nobody that I knew in the military ever thought of it that way. The idea was to have overwhelming strength so that nobody would dare attack us . . . that we would have such strength that we would never have to do any fighting.[20]

One of LeMay's deputies, General Jack J. Catton, who spent sixteen years in SAC, added, "'Massive' referred to what we could do proportionately to what the Russians could do to us. We had nuclear supremacy over the Soviets—such substantial nuclear superiority that it was massive in relation to what they could bring to bear on us. . . . There was a very clear targeting philosophy and a very professional war plan for SAC to go to war. In those early days in the 1950s, SAC was about the only war force we possessed."[21]

If that statement appears parochial, it reflected the reality as seen from Omaha.

CHAPTER 8

SAC: Wielding the Weapon

AFTER THE SIGNING OF THE KOREAN ARMISTICE IN JULY 1953, SAC again turned its full attention to the Soviet threat. At the end of that year LeMay's force numbered 760 bombers, with nearly 330 B-47s. But the command's strength was measured in more than bombers: LeMay called upon some 280 long-range reconnaissance aircraft (mostly RB-36s and –47s) plus 500 KC-97 and KB-29 tankers. With a total of 1,830 aircraft, including escort fighters and heavy-lift transports, SAC was an entity unto itself, larger than many foreign air forces and more capable than most, even without nuclear weapons.

However, building an offensive force was one thing; finding the enemy's most valued assets was another. One of SAC's greatest challenges was targeting, especially the location of Soviet nuclear forces.

Bomber bases and missile silos were therefore of constant interest, especially in the era before satellite surveillance.

Consequently, LeMay gained approval for reconnaissance flights into Soviet and Warsaw Pact countries, gathering photographic and atmospheric intelligence. The "RB" versions of the Peacemaker and Stratojet were the preferred platforms, sniffing around the Communist periphery and frequently penetrating hostile airspace. Some RB-36 crews grew downright complacent, bragging about how much nap time they had over Siberia. But it was a dangerous game: From 1952 to 1965 the air force lost seven recon planes with seventy-nine fliers; the navy lost even more men over a longer period.[1]

One example of what could go wrong occurred during a 1954 mission that snooped northern Russia. The RB-47 crew was briefed that the high-flying Boeing was in no danger from the standard Soviet fighter, the MiG-15.

Abruptly tracers lit up the thin air around the '47. Gouges were hacked out of the aluminum skin as 23mm shells ripped the airframe. The pilot immediately took evasive action, and escaped the Russian fighters—new MiG-17s!

Four months later LeMay decorated the recon airmen. Seemingly almost embarrassed, he said they deserved Silver Stars but that award would draw unwelcome attention, adding, "You've got to explain that to congress and everyone else in Washington, so I'll give you guys Distinguished Flying Crosses instead!"[2]

LeMay's insistence on decorating his fliers was typical, recalling his exceptional effort to get the Medal of Honor for Sergeant Erwin in 1945. The difference, of course, was geopolitical: The B-29 gunner was publicly lauded for exceptional heroism whereas the RB-47 crew remained obscure, owing to the clandestine nature of its mission. But in both cases LeMay took measures to demonstrate his appreciation for his troops

Even in nuclear war planning, the old question still applied: how many bombs were enough?

In 1954 LeMay told the National War College that he preferred to attack Soviet airpower on the ground. Assuming some degree of warning for an actual or intended attack, he favored an immediate response—mutual blows if necessary, but preferably preemptive.[3]

That statement likely indicates U.S. Air Force concern with Russia's massive tactical airpower. In any case, Soviet Long-Range Aviation (LRA) apparently did not possess a nuclear capability until 1956, and even four years later LRA only had about 120 bombers with 350 weapons. SAC, by comparison, possessed some 1,500 nuke-capable aircraft bearing two bombs per airframe: an American superiority of ten or twelve to one at the time of the presidential campaign's focus on "the narrowing bomber gap."

During the 1950s, the balance of strategic forces between America and Russia certainly suited LeMay's professional instincts. As seen from World War II onward, every time he could arrange for a huge advantage in his favor, he seized it. Then he proceeded to build on it, as he did in the Marianas. Given the context of the cold war, it is not surprising that he applied the same process to SAC.

Not surprisingly, the Joint Chiefs of Staff (JCS) chairman Nathan Twining, an airman, sided with LeMay. Understandably, he felt it preferable to destroy a given target in the first attempt, and considered that conditions in a full-scale war required erring on the side of caution.[4]

In the mid-1950s SAC launched a succession of record-setting flights calculated to demonstrate the command's growing capability—and to keep LeMay's force front row center on Capitol Hill. In 1953 a B-47 flew from Loring Air Force Base in Maine to Britain in less than five hours—an average of just over 600 mph with the westerly tailwind. Later that year two B-36s winged from Yokota, Japan, to Loring in twenty-eight and a half hours: a bit more than 10,000 miles for an average 350 mph.

Nor was that all. The next year three B-47s jetted their way from March Air Force Base, California, to Yokota: 6,700 miles non-stop in fifteen hours (nearly 450 mph, against the prevailing winds).

But those were individual or small formation efforts. In 1955 LeMay dispatched two B-47 wings from Florida to "attack" European targets before proceeding to North Africa. Ninety jet bombers were refueled en route, completing the mission as planned. Global reach had become not only possible, but routine.

The next year, 1956, LeMay sent twenty-one B-47 wings on practice missions over the North Pole: eight million combat-capable miles made possible by eighteen tanker squadrons. For all their historic emphasis on mass, the Soviets recognized that they simply could not compete with SAC. That was what Curtis LeMay intended: It was intimidation on a global scale.

It has been said that in order to increase SAC funding, in the mid-1950s LeMay convinced the Eisenhower administration of a "bomber gap" that was not confirmed by other sources. Reportedly the CIA expressed doubts, but available intelligence led the administration to accept LeMay's theory.

It is not possible to say whether LeMay was being disingenuous or cautious in testifying about the bomber gap without knowing what information was available to him. The context of the time—especially the mid- to late 1950s—certainly played a role in creating a climate of concern. In 1954–55 the emergence of Soviet strategic bombers received wide play in the West: the long-lived turboprop Tu-95 (NATO Bear), the jet Tu-16 (NATO Badger), and the lesser known Mya–4 (NATO Bison), the latter mainly employed as a tanker. The Badger was roughly equivalent to the B-47 with similar performance and built in comparable numbers.

Then came *Sputnik* in 1957. Taken together with Soviet expansionism, the credibility for a serious Communist aerospace threat only grew.

Apparently Soviet Premier Kruschev was inclined to exaggerate Russia's capabilities for reasons either practical or prideful, but it is possible that he was misinformed by military subordinates who did not wish to be seen as inferior to the Americans. At any rate, Russia seems to have adopted a "Potemkin village" policy, staking out dummy bombers to be counted by Western observers, and repeatedly flying a few advanced aircraft over May Day parades. At the time, the Russians probably knew more about U.S. strength than Washington did of the Soviet Union's, but neither side was going to show its cards.

Apart from the Soviet bomber threat, SAC and the air force generally became more concerned about Russia's intercontinental ballistic missile (ICBM) programs emerging in the early 1950s. That, in turn, led to more emphasis on reconnaissance.

Some of LeMay's initiatives were astonishing in light of later defenses. On one occasion he sent dozens of recon aircraft in high-speed dashes over Vladivostok "at high noon." Only two planes saw MiGs but no Russian fighters made an interception. CinCSAC concluded, "We practically mapped the place up there with no resistance at all."[5]

The reason for recon, of course, was targeting. LeMay stressed the need for an integrated target list among all the services, based on approximately 2,400 priority aiming points. Roughly one-eighth were duplicates, reflecting a doctrinal emphasis on what World War II airmen called "restrike." Obviously, in a nuclear war there might be little opportunity to return to a target that escaped destruction or retained some capability, which induced air force planners to opt for maximum destruction: multiple attacks and/or high yields. Certainly LeMay's B-29 campaign had run toward maximum efforts, and that philosophy applied to nuclear weapons as well.

LeMay's willingness to challenge the Soviets in their own airspace may seem unnecessarily provocative fifty years later. But it underlines the crucial importance of visual reconnaissance in the days before satellites. It also reinforces SAC's institutional reliance upon intimidation, in even more dramatic form than the long-distance deployments of bomber wings to the periphery of the Soviet Union.

Intimidation worked well within the framework of deterrence, a fact that LeMay seems to have grasped intuitively. However, deterrence could work the other way, as witnessed by America's halfway measures in Vietnam, for fear of a greater Soviet and especially a Chinese response. In today's context, as then, military commanders and their political masters need to recall that no matter how powerful the force structure, there can be no deterrence without credibility.

The overflights of Soviet and Warsaw Pact territory did not occur merely on LeMay's whim, nor anyone else's. President Eisenhower and the joint chiefs supported the reconnaissance efforts, which sometimes reached significant proportions. For instance, in the spring of 1955 SAC launched Project Seashore, employing RB-47s to overfly the Urals. Other flights toured the periphery of the Soviet Union from Alaska and Greenland. Missions by CIA U-2s also increased in 1955–56, so LeMay was certainly not operating in a vacuum.

The overflight climax occurred in May 1960, when a U-2 was shot down over Russia. Soviet Premier Kruschev demanded an apology and an American pledge to stop intrusions into Russian airspace. Dissatisfied with Eisenhower's response, he walked out of a Paris summit, and the cold war turned chillier.

Whatever LeMay's attitude toward such events, undoubtedly his pragmatism ruled. Until the shootdown, U-2 flights had been conducted almost without opposition, and the Soviets' inability to defend the upper regions of their own airspace was an advantage that SAC could not ignore. Just as "restrike" had become a doctrinal tenet in World War II, keeping German factories out of business, so too did return flights to Soviet targets help SAC planners maintain current briefing folders for combat crews.

Living in a constant state of combat readiness, SAC maintained standards that may have appeared severe to outsiders. But LeMay believed there was too much at stake to give a second chance to officers in sensitive positions. "It was war," he insisted, whether any bombs were dropped or not. He had the same attitude toward personnel: "I cannot afford to differentiate between the incompetent and the unfortunate."[6]

In order to check the operational capability of each wing, LeMay sent no-notice inspection teams throughout the command. The team would arrive at a base unannounced and hand the "wing king" a letter from the commander in chief: "Execute your war plan." Typically, the wing launched twelve aircraft that might fly from the United States, conduct radar bombing of a target in France, land in England, and return. Then the profile was repeated.

Despite some draconian methods (spot promotions for an entire crew and reduction in rank for everyone based on an individual's misstep), LeMay was not a micromanager. "I picked people that [sic] could do the job. Then I got out of the way and let him do it. . . . If he did it, fine. If he didn't, I got somebody else."[7]

Apart from operational efficiency, LeMay was equally concerned with airbase security. In fact, he often said that only two things mattered: SAC targets and SAC bases. He probably placed more emphasis on base security than any major air commander in history.

In 1951 LeMay had insisted on a full-time organization devoted to testing SAC bases' ability to protect aircraft and facilities. One of the reasons he instigated the continuous airborne alert status was to avoid having all his bombers caught on the ground, either by a surprise attack or by infiltrators. He operated on the pragmatic assumption that if he could think of a means to get inside, so could the Soviets.

He said, "Throughout the Command we played a lot of cops and robbers, but it wasn't for fun. It was for real."[8]

SAC bases possessed multilayered security forces, from the visible sentries with carbines and attack dogs to random ID checks and covert surveillance. Each level was tested by LeMay's "penetration teams." His security apparatus dispatched all manner of interlopers, including men dressed as air force personnel, as vending machine technicians, letter carriers, even as surveyors. It was potentially deadly work, as armed guards were authorized to shoot, and some team members were badly mauled by Dobermans and German Shepherds. But there was never a shortage of willing "penetrators."

LeMay attributed the stream of volunteers to the very fact that it was dangerous work. He felt that danger lent a sense of romantic adventure in the minds of young men. In one joint exercise with Air Defense Command and the Royal Canadian Air Force, forty cities in North America were "targeted" for air attack while the penetration teams tried to breach SAC security. Eighty percent of the "agents" were captured, though one did leave his calling card: a note left in a B-36 asserting that the Peacemaker had been destroyed.

In an incident that became legendary, two penetrators easily passed a checkpoint at McDill Air Force Base, driving a van disguised as the usual early morning breakfast delivery for the command post. Their badges, complete with photos, identified them as Joseph Stalin and Mickey Mouse. The communist despot and the precocious rodent proceeded to the command post, where they were admitted by personnel awaiting rolls and coffee. The penetrators then handed the duty officer a note stating that he and his personnel were pronounced dead at the scene.

Despite such glitches, or perhaps because of them, security tightened throughout the command. Later evaluation concluded that no more than two percent of penetration attempts succeeded, and far fewer achieved their missions.

LeMay often figured in stories about base security. In one instance he reportedly noted a suspicious phone repairman and held the man at bay with a loaded .45 pistol.

In another episode, allegedly the chief himself drove a truck through a gate, drawing a carbine shot that shattered the rear window. The vehicle screeched to a stop, tires squealing, and the cigar-smoking driver bailed out. Advancing on the sentry, LeMay reportedly congratulated the young airman for his diligence, then demoted him—for missing.

LeMay admitted no recollection of either incident, but neither did he deny them.

Under LeMay, like the rest of SAC, security personnel achieved unprecedented levels of professionalism. No longer were air police merely a visible presence—base traffic cops with armbands and night sticks. Instead, they represented the tip of the security iceberg that extended from the perimeter fence to the center of the command post. The institutional effects proved permanent, and today's air base defense forces trace their heritage to LeMay in the 1950s.

SAC security did not end with base defense. Looking outward to the threat, LeMay wanted the force to be able to absorb a first strike and continue operating in some meaningful capacity. Consequently, he began a two-year project to move his command center into a hardened underground facility, with secure communications and a defensible perimeter.

LeMay's two-sided policy—similar emphasis on offense and defense—still applies half a century later. Commanders in the twenty-first century may look at the vastly changed technological landscape, especially regarding information management and communications, and infer that SAC in the 1950s has little to offer in the way of lessons learned. The fact that SAC itself no longer exists may only reinforce that attitude. But LeMay recognized that without an effective "shield," his long-range "spear" was in danger of reduced effectiveness, which explains his unrelenting insistence upon readiness, the product of preparation and training.

During the cold war, a first strike in either direction was of obvious concern to American planners. But those who advocated a preemptive attack by U.S. strategic forces did so at their own risk. In 1950, shortly after the Korean War began, Major General Orvil Anderson had openly urged America to act "before it is too late," asserting that the air force could destroy Russia's "A-bomb nests" in a week. Almost immediately Anderson was relieved of his command.

In that context, any officer who voiced similar sentiments was skating on very thin ice. Yet, in 1954, LeMay had been asked about a U.S. first strike and characteristically he had spoken his mind, though in a relatively safe air force environment. Noting that current national policy prohibited such action, he summoned his objectivity in recalling that Americans had started their own revolution, the War of 1812, most of the Indian wars, and the Spanish-American War.[9]

+———+

In 1955 SAC was a growth industry. LeMay disposed of twenty-three B-47 wings; six with B 36s; and the first B-52 outfit at Castle AFB. In all, he controlled some 3,000 aircraft, including 1,300 bombers of which 85 percent were B-47 and new B-52 jets.[10]

That year the command became more streamlined as the last SAC fighters returned to Tactical Air Command. As bomber capabilities steadily increased, the perceived need for long-range escorts diminished. When LeMay took command, more than one-quarter of his aircraft were fighters. At the end of 1954 the number of F-84s peaked at 411 but represented barely 15 percent of SAC's total.

Ten years after the end of World War II, U.S. airpower doctrine had come full circle: The bomber was again on its own, without escorts.

The change in force structure reflected increased confidence in SAC's ability to reach its targets. LeMay had assumed command six years previously with an obsolescent fighter component that he upgraded as quickly as possible. But even with new jets, the strategic escort wings proved largely unworkable in the evolving operational world of long-range bombers. Distances to targets were greater than ever before, and the disparity in speeds between bombers and fighters had narrowed considerably. Rather than cling to an outmoded doctrine, the erstwhile fighter pilot adapted to the new reality and refined his command for optimum performance.

LeMay surprised some people with his acceptance of intercontinental ballistic missiles. As the original big bomber man, he was often expected to resist anything that replaced pilots, bombardiers, and navigators. But he said, "I was glad to get missiles. As a matter of fact, some of those things were started when I was in charge of R&D on the air staff."[11]

It was true: LeMay had anticipated the use of long-range missiles during his tour as chief of research and development in the late 1940s. But as he noted much later, technological advances between 1948 and 1957 were erratic, mainly because funding was slow, and SAC did not gain a credible ICBM capability until his tour as vice chief of staff.

The distinction that LeMay drew between bombers and ICBMs was one of confidence. SAC crews performed their functions hundreds of times, achieving unprecedented levels of skill and reliability. That was not possible with missiles: Each ICBM had a potential "sortie rate" of exactly 1.00 and no more. Consequently, there was always a lingering doubt as to how many of the siloed birds would fly when it came time to turn the launch keys. But considering the overall strategic plan—the "big picture"— LeMay welcomed missiles because they added to America's deterrent credibility.

Thor was SAC's first missile, an intermediate range weapon (2,000 miles) that began testing in 1957, a few months before LeMay left SAC. Nevertheless, it set the stage for the true ICBMs that followed.

Some pilots were openly skeptical of ICBMs' accuracy. To fire a missile 5,000 miles and strike within two miles of the aim point seemed beyond reason. But before the end of the cold war, ICBMs were capable of landing within yards of the target.

The factor that LeMay most admired about bombers was their flexibility. Even assuming the perfect ICBM—one button pushed equals one target vaporized—he saw total reliance upon missiles as a musclebound position. ICBMs were naturally all-or-nothing weapons: They sat in their silos or they sped toward their destruction. He said, "You're off the button and we are at peace; or you're on the button and we are at war." Therefore, he compared missiles to a space age Maginot Line.

Perhaps the ultimate expression of the need for pilots came from a naval aviator, X-15 test pilot Scott Crossfield. In the 1960s he exclaimed "There will always be a need for manned aircraft because no other guidance system can be produced so cheaply by unskilled labor."

+━━━◇+

While SAC was growing in strength and confidence, so was the Soviet Union. Supersonic fighters emerged with the MiG-19 in 1955, and the faster, more capable MiG-21 four years later.

Surface-to-air missiles (SAMs) also appeared in the Russian lineup. The SA-1 was deployed around Moscow in 1954 but it was a large, cumbersome weapon retained only for that locale. Three years later the more effective, vastly more long-lived SA-2 appeared in Russia and East Germany. It was built to kill Stratofortresses but became the bane of U-2 pilots and tactical aircrews in Southeast Asia.

LeMay oversaw SAC's response to the increased Russian threat, and his approach reflected his professional experience. His postwar tour as director of research and development had reinforced his confidence in aviation electronics, much as his early exposure to rocketry led to his support of long-range missiles. Consequently, SAC crews increasingly relied upon airborne sensors and jammers to counter enemy defenses, preserve bombers from attack, and get them to their targets. For a longer period than any air commander in history, LeMay had to absorb a near constant stream of operational and technical changes, adapt to new threats and situations, and field appropriate responses. Given the headlong rush of aviation technology, it was a massive challenge yet he seemed to take it in stride.

LeMay's influence in SAC extended well beyond his departure. His primary legacy was leadership, but included significant weapons such as Convair's B-58 Hustler, the world's first supersonic bomber. It was a "LeMay airplane," designed and built during his tenure, whereas he had inherited the B-47 and B-52 programs.

The Hustler began with a 1951 competition between Boeing and Convair to develop the successor to the B-47. Following further design studies, the XB-58 was approved in 1953. The result was a dramatic aerodynamic profile that still looks futuristic in the twenty-first century.

Because of their cost, few B-58s were built—only enough to equip two wings. In 1960 the Forty-third Bomb Wing got the first Hustlers while LeMay's old 305th was equipped the next year. The delta-winged speedster represented more than an advanced bomber—it was symbolic of the headlong rush of aviation progress. The Forty-third's commander, Colonel James K. Johnson, set transcontinental speed records in the Mach 1.6 jet. Two decades before, his first operational aircraft had been the 230-mph Boeing P-26.

Despite its performance, the complex B-58 served only ten years, being retired in 1970. The fact that no Hustler ever flew a combat mission was testament to LeMay's emphasis on maintaining a credible deterrence.

LeMay knew the value of public relations. He did everything possible to extol his command's growing capabilities, in print and in film. He recruited celebrities in his effort and invited reporters not merely to see a B-36 up close, but to experience what it was like to fly a 3,000-mile mission.

In the 1950s most of the news media were happy to cooperate with the military, often on short notice. One example was Operation Quick Kick in 1957, a LeMay counterattack against a series of articles critical of the B-52. He learned that a freelance reporter, P. D. Eldred, had compiled detailed information about the Stratofort's early failings, partly by interviewing personnel and families at Castle Air Force Base, California.

The timing was poor from SAC's perspective. About the same time, LeMay had to inform Congress that nearly half of the first seventy-eight B-52s were rejected for deficient parts. On top of that, two bombers had been lost with fatalities, leading to the Strato fleet temporarily being grounded and prompting calls for a congressional investigation. When LeMay learned of Eldred's upcoming series, he launched Quick Kick.

The timing could hardly have been better. On January 16, 1957, five Boeings departed Castle on a round-the-world flight. Quick Kick's lead ship was christened *Lucky Lady III,* maintaining the name of previous globe-trotting bombers, and though two aborted, the others circled the earth, sustained by some ninety KC-97 tankers. Upon return to base, the triumphant fliers had cut the circumnavigation to barely forty-five hours. Two days later, amid laudatory press coverage, *Lucky Lady's* crew rode in Eisenhower's inaugural parade.

Eldred's wire service articles ran as scheduled, but garnered little attention. LeMay, SAC, and the B-52 proceeded on course.[12]

From 1948 through 1965, Hollywood produced nearly forty films depicting the air force from World War II into the present—or near future. Though personally averse to publicity, LeMay gave full support to patriotic or recruiting movies depicting the service—and especially SAC—in a favorable light. They included *Strategic Air Command* (1955) with air force reservist Jimmy Stewart and the ever-sweet June Allyson as a baseball family caught up in the cold war. LeMay is a factor in the person of cigar-chomping General Hawks, played by perennial tough guy Frank Lovejoy. From a SAC perspective the film traces the conversion from B-36s (filmed in gorgeous Technicolor) to B-47s.

Other LeMay-backed films included *Bombers B-52* (1957) and *A Gathering of Eagles* (1963). In the *Steve Canyon* television series

(1958–60) the hero flew nearly everything in the inventory at "Big Thunder Air Force Base."

One PR coup was directly attributed to LeMay, SAC's signature motto, "Peace is our profession." It was vintage LeMay: terse and cogent, emphasizing the command's mission of deterrence.

In return, fighter pilots swilled their "suds" at happy hour and boasted, "Hell, *war* is our profession!"

+=—=+

In the 1950s LeMay cultivated the friendship of entertainer Arthur Godfrey, who enjoyed an immense following on radio and television. A former navy radioman and reserve commander, Godfrey was one of America's leading aviation boosters and seldom missed an opportunity to plug navy air. Once in LeMay's grasp, the media maestro was treated to a worldwide look at SAC operations. He was suitably impressed, and then some. He resigned from the naval reserve in favor of a "blue suit" commission. It was a major coup for LeMay and the air force.

SAC's public relations efforts took unusual turns for a military organization. For instance, as a devoted sports car driver, LeMay was aware that open-road racing was waning in America. Sections of public highway were increasingly restricted during the 1950s, prompted by some well-publicized tragedies. Consequently, LeMay decided to open some SAC bases for road races with courses laid out on lengthy runways. The decision proved enormously popular with racing fans.

Nothing would do but for SAC to field its own racing team. The original drivers were LeMay with Colonel David Schilling, commander of the Thirty-first Fighter Escort Wing, and SAC's public relations officer, Colonel Reade Tilley. Ironically, both were hardcore fighter pilots, aces of World War II. Schilling earned a sterling reputation commanding the Fifty-sixth Group Thunderbolts in

England while Tilley, originally an Eagle Squadron pilot, flew Spitfires at Malta.

Tilley was the right man in the right job. A big, garrulous Texan, he exuded disarming charm in social events and a tigerish aggressiveness on the track. He was highly popular with the public, proving a valuable asset and counterpoint to LeMay's gruff, often foreboding demeanor.

Schilling, a sure thing for general, fell victim to his love of racing. He was killed driving a sports car in Britain in 1956.

In 1954 LeMay dipped into his stash of old friends and got Lieutenant General Francis H. Griswold to succeed Power as deputy SAC commander. LeMay and Griswold had served together forever: flying school, Hawaii, and Britain. Excepting their long association, Griswold was a surprise choice to relieve Power, never having served in SAC. In fact, most of his previous service had been in fighters and ordnance or material positions. Nonetheless, "Butch" Griswold was a popular deputy commander, possessing far more people skills than "Tommy" Power, who moved on to R&D.

Griswold was one of those few people who thoroughly understood LeMay. They were completely comfortable together, often passing hours without exchanging a word. Their wives marveled at the mutually taciturn airmen whose friendship seemed based more upon mental telepathy than conversation.

However, communications figured prominently in the LeMay-Griswold scheme of things. When Griswold arrived at Offutt he found the commander in chief absorbed with improving command and control by any means available. Consequently, the deputy commander joined his boss in obtaining a private radio license, and together they began exploring the amateur frequency bands. Most of the bands were clogged with other amateur radio operators, but the two persisted. Eventually they came upon the single sideband (SSB) option and built a set for experimentation. SSB was inherently more discrete than the common bands, and lent itself to encryption technology. Consequently, ignoring air force regulations (after all, they wore seven stars between them), LeMay had their set installed in an aircraft that Griswold flew to Japan.

Back in Omaha, LeMay kept in voice contact with his deputy and was pleasantly surprised at the relative clarity and reliability of the side-band set. Thus began a lengthy campaign against the air force communications bureaucracy, which was perhaps understandably reluctant to admit that a set built by a couple of generals offered better performance than vastly more expensive government equipment. LeMay got around the official barriers by diverting some operating funds to a dozen side-band sets that he deployed abroad: from Newfoundland to the Azores, Britain, Morocco, and elsewhere. After a period of demonstrated success, the air force yielded to the LeMay-Griswold team and adopted high-frequency side-band radios throughout the service.

+>———<+

In 1957, when LeMay departed SAC to become vice chief of staff, his successor was easily anticipated. Thomas Power had been deputy commander for LeMay's first six years in SAC, moving to air research and development for three years. In pilot slang, Power "shook the stick," relieving his erstwhile boss, and figuratively moving into SAC's left seat.

Power was, by all reckonings, bright and capable but was widely considered "a mean SOB." LeMay was all too aware of Power's "personality problems" but trusted his judgment and ability, having worked intimately with him in XXI Bomber Command as well as SAC's formative years.[13]

LeMay left SAC in excellent condition: 224,000 personnel (nearly 30,000 officers) with 2,700 aircraft, including 768 tankers. The force was approaching 100 percent jet bombers and recon aircraft with the first KC-135 jet tankers arriving to augment 740 piston-engined KC-97.

However, LeMay did not always make use of available assets. He was adamantly opposed to Air National Guard units in SAC, as they were subject to control by their respective states. That arrangement was not always conducive to SAC requirements, and LeMay only wanted units that he could plan on using. With Air Guard KC-97s supporting Tactical Air Command, the SAC leadership often resented a tanker capability beyond their control.

An Arizona guardsman said, "It wasn't until he left the scene that we got tankers. It was truly LeMay's Air Force."[14]

Nevertheless, with 1948 as a baseline, LeMay increased personnel by four and a half times and aircraft by a magnitude of three. But there were other lasting improvements, many less tangible, including food and housing, promotions, and retention. The greatest factor in LeMay's leadership, the sum of the foregoing, was morale. From a force largely in name only, SAC became the premier military organization on the planet. Its standards and professionalism—its pride in itself—were the doings of Curtis LeMay.

Though LeMay held the world's largest nuclear stick, like every commander he only wielded what his nation provided him. At that time the U.S. strategic inventory was over 5,500 warheads, including more than 2,000 strategic. The Soviets still lagged with 650, including 100 strategic.[15]

In order to allocate its assets, SAC had developed the Air Power Battle Target System involving 1,439 communist targets, of which 954 were marked for immediate attack: nuclear storage and production facilities, strategic bomber fields, and command and control centers, with long-range missiles also gaining attention. LeMay oversaw the system's creation, providing for updates as required—yet another legacy that he ceded to his successors.[16]

LeMay's nine years as CinCSAC remained the longest tenure in a major command since Winfield Scott's term as "general in chief" of the army (1841–61). When he left Omaha for Washington,

LeMay might have suspected that he had concluded his life's work. He had molded SAC into his image: tough, capable, and professional, but there was little likelihood that he could effect similar changes in the air force. For one thing, the other commands already were mature entities; for another, he would not have nearly a decade to bring his influence to bear.

For Curtis LeMay, life in Washington, D.C. would never be as satisfying as his work with SAC. Nothing else in his life so thoroughly defined him.

CHAPTER 9

Washington

IN JULY 1957 LEMAY HAD BEEN COMMANDER OF THE
Strategic Air Command for nine years. Now he was second in command of the entire U.S. Air Force.

LeMay's selection as vice chief for General Thomas D. White
was an obvious one, but not without some concern in official circles.
Despite LeMay's seniority and undeniable qualifications, the two
generals' personalities were worlds apart.

White was four years older than LeMay and a West Pointer to
boot. As an airman he could not begin to compete with LeMay's
cockpit experience, White's only tactical assignment being an observation squadron during the 1920s. However, White was polished
and worldly, with extensive diplomatic experience as a military attaché in China, Russia, Italy, and Brazil. He spent most of World

War II in the States but went to the Pacific in 1944–45 with senior positions in the Seventh and Thirteenth Air Forces.

LeMay and White were colleagues, not friends. They had briefly met in South America in 1941 when White was air attaché to Brazil, and apart from their different personalities, they had very few interests in common. For one thing, LeMay still enjoyed flying, even as a four-star. His devotion to hunting, fishing, and shooting set him apart from many of his contemporaries.

More significant was the two officers' differing approach to problem solving. With a sophisticated world view, White was open to suggestions of compromise on most issues. In vivid contrast, LeMay tended to see compromise as capitulation and said, "Tommy wouldn't get down in the mud and fight."[1]

Yet the two worked well together. White necessarily devoted most of his time to matters on the joint chiefs, leaving LeMay to run the air force. It would have been relatively easy for the vice chief to do largely as he wished and force the chief to rubber stamp a fait accompli, but LeMay recognized his obligation to his superior and to the service. Whenever he was in doubt about White's preferences, he awaited an opportunity to discuss matters in private. Such diplomacy did not go unnoticed.

One of the first issues LeMay found awaiting him was a requested pay increase for air force personnel—and by extension, to everyone in uniform. Toward that end, he accompanied the Second Air Force commander, General John P. McConnell, to meet informally with the most powerful man on Capitol Hill—senate majority leader Lyndon B. Johnson.

The two generals flew to Texas for a weekend with Johnson, trying to cajole him to support a 6.5 percent pay raise. Johnson claimed he was sympathetic to the request but insisted that it could not pass either house or Congress. He spent the first night giving the visitors a pickup tour of the area, drinking whiskey while driving to visit local ranchers. LeMay was not impressed.

Having been rebuffed in Texas, LeMay called for reinforcements in the form of Arthur Godfrey. The media star invited Johnson to a private party and made the same pitch as the air force men, with the same result. Johnson said that without grassroots support, the pay increase was dead on arrival.

Arthur Godfrey informed millions of listeners of the lamentable situation in America's armed forces and suggested that they make their preferences known. LeMay knew that listeners equaled voters who equaled political power. Several months later, Eisenhower signed the military pay raise into law.

***

On October 4, 1957, the Russians stunned the world—to say nothing of the U.S. Air Force—by launching a satellite into Earth orbit. Though technologically a relatively minor feat, *Sputnik* began circling the Earth, beeping its foreboding signals, and the echoes resonated in America's halls of power. The Soviets soon followed their feat with a second success thirty days later, carrying a shepherd dog.

In describing Washington's reaction, one officer said, "Everybody went spastic." Two months passed before America got *Explorer 1* off the launch pad.

For SAC the result was increased readiness. General Power had 1,528 bombers and 766 tankers at the time, and placed 11 percent on operational alert. That meant 170 bombers and 84 refuelers, a figure that increased to 20 percent two years later.

Recognizing the PR crisis, LeMay sought ways of retrieving some of the American public's lost confidence.

On Veteran's Day LeMay took off from Westover Air Force Base, Massachusetts, in a KC-135, bound for South America. Ostensibly his mission was to deliver President Eisenhower's congratulations to the new president of Argentina. The Stratotanker was stuffed with fuel and reporters who provided exactly what LeMay actually wanted: a counterpoint to Russia's space achievement and a demonstration of SAC's global reach. The Soviets could read a map: They recognized that the 6,322 miles from Westover to Buenos Aires was less than the distance over the pole from DC to Murmansk in northern Russia. The 5,200-mile return flight to Washington, D.C., took eleven hours, averaging 472 mph.

Subsequently LeMay received the Harmon Trophy for outstanding international aviation achievements. Of the nine Harmons since World War II, LeMay's was the eighth to an American, the seventh to an air force man.

The honor meant far less than the fact that he continued flying whenever possible. Almost a year after the Buenos Aires trip he flew another tanker from Tokyo to Washington, setting a record in the process. Because of the time zones, he arrived a half-hour after leaving.

<hr>

In 1959 Russia established the Strategic Rocket Forces (SRF), a separate military service. While LeMay had no direct Soviet counterpart commanding both bombers and missiles, the threat was looming. Over the next five years the Russians deployed submarine-launched missiles as well as increasingly capable land-based weapons—all of growing concern to LeMay and the U.S. Air Force.

Even allowing for America's later Strategic Integrated Operational Plan (SIOP), the Soviet Union possessed greater integration and command of its strategic weapons than the United States. Post–cold war orthodoxy aside, Curtis LeMay never commanded all of America's nuclear arsenal. That privilege was reserved for whatever politician resided at 1600 Pennsylvania Avenue.

Amid Washington's concern about growing Soviet capabilities emerged a revolutionary design: North American Aviation's B-70 bomber. Dating from a 1955 high-speed concept, it was unlike anything yet flown, and more than a generation beyond the B-58. With

Mach three speed and very high altitude—over 70,000 feet—the B-70 was expected to operate beyond the limits of current Russian fighters and air-defense missiles. LeMay wanted it. Named the Valkyrie, the futuristic design featured prominently in LeMay's professional wish list.

However, as the flying generals were learning, the most pertinent battles were fought not in the stratosphere but at ground level in Washington, D.C.

In 1960 the U.S. Navy achieved operational status with its first Polaris-armed ballistic missile submarine. It was a welcome addition, expanding the nuclear deterrence triad into a reality, but LeMay believed that the submariners were claiming more than they could deliver.

The nuclear-powered missile subs (SSBNs) enjoyed one great advantage over land-based aircraft and missiles: relative invulnerability. Cruising in the depths of the world's oceans, they were extremely difficult to detect and therefore ensured that the Soviets could not eliminate a majority of American strategic weapons in one massive strike.

By the late 1950s SAC had approximately 5,500 "aim points" representing Soviet, Warsaw Pact, and Chinese targets. But as the target list grew, neither SAC nor the navy's new ballistic-missile submarines could reach them all. LeMay and the air force were faced with a new situation: having to share the nuclear menu with the naval partner at the strategic table.

In order to avoid target duplication, the air force and navy developed the integrated plan, assigning specific targets to SAC bombers and ICBMs as well as submarine-launched missiles. The plan was drafted in 1960 and continuously updated thereafter.

In 1962 the Rand Corporation studied the SIOP, identifying a doomsday menu serving up 3,200 warheads against Communist targets worldwide. By some estimates, the massive strike could have inflicted 250 million casualties. However, the next year defense secretary Robert McNamara changed American nuclear strategy away from cities and factories, concentrating largely upon "counterforce" targets: Soviet missile sites and bomber bases.

Whatever the targeting policy, LeMay and other air force leaders noted that the submarine's very advantage—mobility—worked against it. In the days before precision satellite navigation, a sub's position might only be approximately known. That in turn affected the accuracy of sub-launched missiles, which had smaller warheads and less range than ICBMs—between 1,000 and 1,500 miles.

The Polaris's cost-benefit tradeoff also compared poorly to land-based systems because at least half of available submarines were either in transit to their operating areas or refitting in port. In contrast, the huge majority of SAC bombers and missiles were available at a given moment.

However, a Pacific Command staffer noted air force concern for due credit in event of a nuclear war. Said then-Commander Donald Gordon, who had helped create the SIOP with other officers, "The Air Force was concerned that the subs would get credit for destroying targets before its systems could get there. LeMay did not want the tactical aircraft in his way when headed for Western or Eastern Russia. But the Fifth and Thirteenth Air Force and Navy carrier aircraft could make two strikes before the B-52s ever got there. The SAC and sub missiles would all be expended before even the Pacific tactical aircraft completed their first flight."[2]

Whatever the merits of either case, none of LeMay's arguments had any effect: The influence of the Navy's nuclear-power community grew tremendously, eventually reaching the point that successive noncombatant officers became chiefs of naval operations. It was a situation unique to the Navy, occurring only once each in the army and air force and never in the marines.

Firearms had been a LeMay passion since childhood. It was a passion he carried throughout his life, yielding long-term effects on the army and Marine Corps.

On July 4, 1960, LeMay was invited to a birthday party for Fairchild's president, Richard Boutelle. During the festivities LeMay was shown the new AR-15 rifle made by Fairchild's Armalite division. He could not pass up the chance to test the .223 caliber weapon on suitable ballistic media: three watermelons. The chief of staff popped the first at 50 yards and the second at 150, saving the survivor for the revelers.

Impressed with the AR's composite materials and design, LeMay asked Boutelle to provide samples for testing. With the air force's inventory of World War II carbines approaching obsolescence, the Armalite offered obvious advantages.

Eventually the air force ordered 80,000 AR-15s in a multiyear contract. The Armalite was produced by Colt as the M16, becoming the standard U.S. infantry weapon. However, the army ordnance bureaucracy made unwarranted changes to Eugene Stoner's innovative weapon, and the "black rifle" took decades to overcome a poor start.

It is ironic to consider LeMay's two greatest equipment legacies: very different weapons at opposite ends of the spectrum. The B-52, which he placed into service in 1954, still flies more than fifty years later. Similarly, the M16, adapted in 1964, still equips the U.S. Army and Marine Corps, with no likely replacement in sight.

Meanwhile, LeMay never lost his fascination with gadgets. His boyhood passion for building crystal radio sets and repairing firearms gradually grew to previously undreamt-of heights. As a general he still tinkered, producing a variety of appliances, including a stereo sound system with speakers positioned throughout the house.

Helen insisted that his crowning achievement was a color television produced in about two months' worth of evenings and Sundays.

But hobbies were transitory; the job was perennial. During the 1960s the on-again, off-again XB-70 Valkyrie featured prominently in the presidential campaign. Amid Democrat charges that the United States was lagging in strategic bomber development, and widening concern over the perceived missile gap, a Mach three intercontinental bomber became a horse worth backing. The Republican nominee, Vice President Richard M. Nixon, was unable to deflect concern expressed by Senator John F. Kennedy, who won a narrow victory that November. LeMay remained a firm advocate of the XB-70, and continued to clash with the Kennedys and their acolytes about the revolutionary, high speed aircraft.

Two operational achievements occurred in February 1961, shortly before LeMay became chief of staff. Both were notable Boeing successes. On February 1, the initial Minuteman ICBM was launched from the Cape Canaveral Missile Test Annex. It arced 4,600 miles downrange to impact in the target area, the first time an unproven missile had been launched with all systems and stages functioning.

Two days later SAC's EC-135 airborne command post became operational. Code named "Looking Glass," the flying control centers mirrored existing ground-based command posts directing air force bombers and ICBMs in event of a successful first strike against Washington, Omaha, and other centers. At the heart of the concept was the vastly reduced response time in the missile era. Presumably enemy bombers could not penetrate North America's air defense zone without giving an hour or more notice. With missiles arriving over the polar ice cap, that figure dropped to fifteen minutes. Consequently, at least one Looking Glass aircraft remained airborne for the next twenty-nine years, and maintained ground or airborne alerts until 1998.

LeMay fought and lost many battles in Washington, usually for approval of equipment and programs that he advocated. Ironically, one of his early defeats involved acquisition of an airplane that he opposed.

Secretary of Defense Robert Strange McNamara was determined to force a new one-size-fits-all aircraft upon the services: air force, navy, and marines. The concept was called TFX, for experimental tactical fighter. Few aviators had much confidence in the idea, which became known as "The Flying Edsel" for McNamara's tenure as head of Ford Motor Company.

In early 1961, nine contractors were invited to submit proposals for TFX and eight complied. However, the next year the air force and navy turned down all the designs, inviting manufacturers to resubmit. In November 1962 General Dynamics (based in Lyndon Johnson's Texas) was selected as the contractor.

The airplane that became the F-111 was a cornerstone of the McNamara regime's passion for jointness. Despite the attractive concept of a swing-wing aircraft capable of doubling as a fighter and bomber, aviators and operators quickly recognized the F-111B's failings. It was too large and underpowered with marginal slow-speed handling for a carrier aircraft.

About that time Lieutenant General David Burchinal, then regarded by some as the best mind in the air force, gave a two-hour presentation describing plans to lengthen the F-111 into the FB-111 tactical fighter-bomber. LeMay sat through the entire briefing without uttering one syllable. When Burchinal finished, LeMay merely said, "It isn't big enough."

In those four words LeMay crammed twelve pounds of analysis into a ten-pound bag. As events demonstrated, the "Aardvark" (for its long nose) airframe was too small for the amount of fuel, ordnance, and systems necessary to perform its intended mission.[3]

Near the end of his tour as vice chief, LeMay played a peripheral role in the first of two Cuban crises, which became known as the Bay of Pigs.

In April 1961 a CIA-sponsored "brigade" of 1,300 anticommunist exiles landed on Cuba's southern coast with the intent of initiating a popular uprising against communist dictator Fidel Castro.

LeMay only learned of the operation a month beforehand, and then by chance. Attending a Joint Chiefs meeting to represent General White, who was traveling, LeMay was astonished when an unidentified civilian described the invasion plan, including air support. The briefer, never introduced but undoubtedly a CIA planner, asked the chiefs their thoughts on the best location for an airfield. The discussion ended with generals and admirals musing over the problem, but LeMay heard little more until April 16, the day before the landings.

LeMay considered the plan haphazard, grossly optimistic, and perhaps worst of all, amateurish. Limited airpower was based in Guatemala and Nicaragua, and given the poor state of Cuban aviation, air superiority might have been achieved. But at the last minute, Secretary of State Dean Rusk cancelled the insurgents' air strikes, leaving the small invasion force wide open to attack. LeMay was appalled. He told a Rusk aide, "You just cut the throats of everybody on the beach."[4]

At Bahia de Cochinos the *insurrectos* were overwhelmed, the survivors captured and eventually ransomed, and "Bay of Pigs" became a synonym for disaster. However, the Kennedy spin machine immediately went to work, and forty years later the conventional wisdom still holds: the young president, who inherited the plan from Eisenhower, had received poor military advice.

Nothing galled Curtis LeMay more than the spurious charge that he or anyone else in uniform had rendered poor advice. Indeed, he knew from personal experience that the military was barely consulted since the fiasco was a CIA operation. It was apparent to him that the plan had little chance to succeed with friendly aircraft, and none at all without, yet Kennedy pressed ahead even though security leaks had occurred days before.

Later it was learned that although U.S. naval airpower was available, carrier pilots orbiting offshore had been prohibited from engaging Castro's fighter-bombers. In LeMay's opinion, Camelot's charming prince and his minions had failed their gut check, and the general would neither forgive nor forget the politicians' folly.

<hr>

On June 30, 1961, Curtis LeMay was named chief of staff and assumed command of the world's most destructive organization. To a large extent he had forged the weapon himself, or at least its most visible component.

While chief of staff, LeMay oversaw fruition of the ICBM program that traced its roots to his time commanding air force research and development. He worked with—and gave most of the credit to—Brigadier General Bernard Schriever, a German-born erstwhile bomber pilot who possessed the energy and ability to push missiles into operational status. Like LeMay, he had survived the 1934 airmail debacle, left the service to earn an engineering degree, and was recalled in 1938. After the war he was selected as the service's liaison officer with the emerging scientific and technological communities—the right man in the right position. Later he became director of the manned orbiting laboratory.

Despite his bomber orientation, SAC missiles became operational during LeMay's final Washington tour: the intermediate range Thor in 1957 and the truly intercontinental Atlas in 1959. The Atlas was operational for the last five years of LeMay's career and featured prominently in America's space program.

The third missile on LeMay's watch was Titan, deployed in 1962 and the first ICBM housed in hardened underground silos. Finally, Minuteman arrived that same year: a much smaller, solid fuel missile that remains in service today.

LeMay never would have denied his bomber prejudice, but he properly defended his progressive record in bringing ICBMs into SAC's inventory. However, on his watch the air force's ability to fight a conventional war left something to be desired. Apparently LeMay regarded Korea as an aberration—a one-time absurdity in which the United States pulled its punches and accepted a draw against a minor enemy when a win had been possible. Surely America would never repeat such folly.

Unfortunately, LeMay found himself a stranger in Camelot, and a not entirely welcome one at that. He arrived in the newfound political landscape six months after John F. Kennedy took office and spent the next four years wandering largely alone, trying to learn the lay of the land.

<hr/>

As chief of staff, LeMay was a marked change from General White. The consummate airman, LeMay was very much a duck out of water in the Byzantine Washington labyrinth where blunt honesty was a liability. In the end, White proved a more adept politician than his successor, but LeMay had to deal with a different situation in a new, progressive Democrat administration. His term on the Joint Chiefs of Staff would be marked by perennial turmoil.

In 1961 LeMay had been a general officer for eighteen years. Of the nine other service chiefs or chairmen during his tenure, only army men Lyman L. Lemnitzer and Maxwell D. Taylor exceeded that record. In fact, LeMay outranked six of his colleagues by a decade or more.

Chief among LeMay's contemporaries was army General Maxwell D. Taylor, an officer with a foot in both military and political worlds. Innovative and intelligent, a distinguished paratroop commander in World War II, he had been chairman under Eisenhower, with whom he disagreed on nuclear strategy.

Taylor had retired in 1959 but remained well connected and politically ambitious. In June 1961 he was appointed to fill a new position, "military representative to the president," effectively circumventing the Joint Chiefs. But it did not take long before he was back in official control: Kennedy recalled him as chairman of the joint chiefs in 1962–64.

Despite his combat credentials, Taylor proved a huge disappointment to many officers when he developed sycophantic tendencies toward his new political masters. Worse, he proved consistently duplicitous toward his fellow chiefs.

✦

Relations between the chiefs and the secretary of defense began as chilly and soon developed a frost. None were frostier than those with the air force chief of staff.

Robert S. McNamara already knew LeMay. During World War II Lieutenant Colonel McNamara had helped establish the AAF Office of Statistical Control at Harvard and had visited B-29 units. He observed LeMay at close range, admiring the general's easy command of his profession and noting the airman's terse gruffness. Whatever he thought of LeMay personally, McNamara reported that XXI Bomber Command was doing more with less: LeMay was getting more airframe hours out of his B-29s than training units in the States. McNamara later said that LeMay was the finest combat commander he had ever met.[5]

Nevertheless, in the 1960s McNamara could tolerate only so much honesty. Knowing that most of the chiefs disagreed with his philosophy and policies, he began representing his own opinions to Johnson as if they were shared by the chiefs.

Curtis Emerson LeMay and Robert Strange McNamara had almost nothing in common other than American citizenship. Their world views could not have been more different. LeMay had contributed to winning World War II by massive application of airpower against Nazi Germany and Imperial Japan. Moreover, he wielded the threat of thermonuclear extermination over the Soviet Union via his bombers and ICBMs. He knew no other way of waging war, even after the Korean stalemate. LeMay's character was shaped by his Midwestern origins and professional experience, characterized by a blunt, un-nuanced honesty and a demonstrated willingness to commit apocalyptic violence in response to overt aggression.

McNamara, on the other hand, looked through his rimless glasses at a world full of shadings and nuances. He believed in gradualism, a tit-for-tat reaction to hostile moves to avoid a sudden escalation of tensions that might prompt Curt LeMay to flush the atomic birds from their hardened coops. The phrase that McNamara laid upon his philosophy was "flexible response." His character arose from a supreme confidence in his Harvard Business School infallibility. Unaccustomed to being challenged, he advised subordinates to answer a reporter's unwelcome question by responding to the question they *wished* had been asked. Such disingenuousness contrasted vividly with LeMay's typical bluntness.[6]

Among other things, LeMay disagreed with the Kennedy administration about nuclear strategy. Most notably, McNamara flatly rejected the concept of a preemptive nuclear strike. In 1967 he said, "The cornerstone of our strategic policy continues to be to deter deliberate nuclear attack upon the United States or its allies by maintaining a highly reliable ability to inflict an unacceptable degree of damage upon any single aggressor or combination of aggressors at any time during the course of a strategic nuclear exchange, even after our absorbing a surprise first strike."[7]

At the same time McNamara noted the disparity between American and Soviet nuclear strength, assuming that the balance of power would deter a Russian initiative.

In the nuclear arena, LeMay fought and lost two notable battles early in his tenure as chief of staff. First was the B-52 replacement, with North American's XB-70. Six turbojets of 31,000 pounds thrust propelled the behemoth bomber to Mach three at 72,000 feet with a 4,200-mile range. However, avoiding high-altitude surface-to-air missiles (SAMs) at Mach three was not possible: The immense G-loads would rip the airframe apart. Lacking a credible low-level capability, the Valkyrie was cancelled in 1961 though the two prototypes were to be retained for high speed research.

The other program was Skybolt, a 1.2 megaton air-launched missile with a 1,100-mile range. In 1959 Douglas was selected as the prime contractor and the next year the air force decided to proceed with deployment, scheduled for 1964. Operational use would have been four missiles carried externally by B-52s, permitting SAC crews to destroy targets from well beyond enemy defenses. LeMay was impressed. So was the Royal Air Force, which committed to purchase as many as 100, modernizing its strategic potential since Britain's aging Avro Vulcan bombers probably could not survive as "penetrators." However, McNamara was opposed to Skybolt (he did not want more strategic weapons in the West) and Kennedy accepted the secretary's opinion. Five unpowered tests were failures but ironically the program was cancelled on the day Skybolt was successfully flown in December 1962.

General David A. Burchinal, who retired as deputy commander of U.S. European forces, shared LeMay's opinion that McNamara had little regard for SAC. Burchinal spoke for many air force officers when he said, "As a matter of fact, he didn't approve any substantial improvements or new weapons for SAC in his budgets, except for Lockheed's SR-71 for reconnaissance. He was the one who sold out the British strategic air forces when he denied them the Skybolt missile, because he wanted to have Britain and France stand down their nuclear forces so there would be a bipolar nuclear world."[8]

Ultimately, McNamara added more submarines and ICBMs to the inventory while improving command and communications—a technical advantage that also permitted micromanagement of the warfighters.

LeMay was bitterly disappointed at both the B-70 and Skybolt defeats, which he regarded as further proof that the Kennedy-Mc-Namara crowd was soft on defense. However, though he spoke plainly in closed hearings on the hill, he kept his own counsel in public, maintaining his philosophy that once an argument had been made and lost, dissent should end.

Meanwhile, America needed a Mach three reconnaissance aircraft, and LeMay knew where to look. Despite his early mistrust of the U-2, he respected Lockheed's superb record, and the fabled "skunk works" produced the A-12 interceptor, which first flew in 1962. The follow-on SR-71 "Blackbird" flew in 1964 and set one record after another.

Forty Blackbirds (designated A-12, YF-12, and SR-71) were built and twenty were lost in accidents from 1963–72, none to enemy action. It remained a LeMay legacy to the air force and the nation.

⊹⟩══⟨⊹

Popular history holds that the world teetered on the brink of annihilation for two weeks in October of 1962, and was rescued at the last minute. However, LeMay and most of his colleagues saw things quite differently. They viewed John F. Kennedy's response to Soviet adventurism not as a diplomatic victory, but as a military defeat.

The signs of impending crisis were evident well ahead of the event. In late May Marshal S. S. Biryuzov, commander of Russia's Strategic Rocket Forces, arrived in Cuba to view possible launch sites. Then, in early September, a Soviet ship offloaded medium-range ballistic missiles (MRBMs) in Havana with a second load following a week later.

U-2s practically camped overhead Cuba during those days, and on October 14 a pilot returned with photos of an MRBM site near

San Cristobal. Additional reconnaissance showed that the Russians were constructing nine missile sites: six for SS-4s and three for the more capable SS-5s. For the moment, the Kennedy clan withheld the information from most military officers.

The SS-5 was Russia's latest missile. With a range of nearly 2,800 miles, it delivered a warhead of more than one megaton. The somewhat older SS-4 could strike targets 1,200 miles distant.

Depending upon their launch position in Cuba, SS-4s could reach an arc from Washington to St. Louis to San Antonio while SS-5s covered all the United States and much of Canada. When recon photos showed Soviet missile bases in Cuba, LeMay was on a European inspection trip. His seat on the joint chiefs was occupied by the vice chief, General William F. McKee.

"Bozo" McKee was indeed a rare bird: the only four-star general as of that time who did not wear pilot's wings. LeMay surprised some by reckoning that a logistician and nonrated vice chief might be an asset, and he was proven correct. McKee had taken office only three months before.

The immediate problem was recalling LeMay from Europe without alerting anyone to the growing emergency. Therefore, McKee called LeMay and said that Congress was about to end the B-70 program. The chief of staff was on the next westbound aircraft, fuming at the "news." The next morning McKee explained the reason for the ruse by saying "We're about to get in a war."[9]

On October 18 the joint chiefs met with Kennedy, who heretofore had relied almost wholly on civilian advice. The service chiefs agreed that military action was necessary, but could not agree on what form it should take. A naval blockade—a "quarantine" in polite terms—was the safest but few felt that it would be effective because the Soviets already had sophisticated weapons ashore: MiG fighters, SAMs, and nuclear rockets. McKee had favored invasion as the only sure way of ousting the threat. LeMay agreed, preferably with an unlimited bombing campaign, as he was confident that massive U.S. nuclear superiority would compel a Soviet withdrawal.

At the time, America possessed 27,000 nuclear warheads while Russia barely had 3,000; the strategic figures were 3,400 to 480. Small wonder that LeMay and some other military leaders were confident that Kruschev would back down. The missile crisis, they reckoned, was hopelessly hyped. America enjoyed a nine-to-one overall superiority and seven-to-one advantage in strategic weapons.

Still, Kennedy was cautious. He doubted that the Russians would take a scouring in Cuba without reacting elsewhere—likely Berlin. LeMay disagreed. Knowing that the nuclear balance of power was overwhelmingly in America's favor, he did not believe that the communist pragmatists in the Kremlin would risk incineration over a Caribbean dictator.

On October 22 Kennedy addressed the nation on television, stating that any missile launch from Cuba would be considered to have come from Russia. He added that the same applied to any aggression in Europe—meaning West Germany.

When the president made that speech, SAC had nuclear-armed B-52s airborne around the clock. The tentative air force response was pure LeMay: massive application of force. In case the Russians would not withdraw, plans were drafted for 160 nuclear weapons (90 tactical) to be dropped on Cuba, delivered by bombers and fighter-bombers.[10]

Recon flights continued apace, with U-2s plus low-flying air force RF-101 Voodoos and naval RF-8 Crusaders. Many were subjected to gunfire but only one was downed: Major Rudolf Anderson's U-2 on October 27. Though Kruschev had ordered no SAM launches, a battery commander either ignored orders or (according to some sources) complied with a directive from Castro himself. In any case, Anderson was the only American casualty of the "thirteen days."

It is not certain that LeMay issued bland assurances that the air force could destroy every missile site. Later he said, "We didn't know whether we had found them all, but we were on alert everyplace and we made sure the Russians understood this."[11]

However logical LeMay's assessment of Soviet priorities regarding Cuba, there was more to be considered. Minor players with their fingers on atomic triggers included Russian submarine captains with nuclear-tipped torpedoes in Cuban waters; the Soviet commander in Cuba with discretion to use tactical weapons; and American fighter pilots with Genie missiles protecting U-2s from MiGs over the Bering Sea. Any of those could conceivably have initiated a wider, if not cataclysmic, war.

The showdown was resolved when Russia agreed to remove the missiles and, far less publicly, America took its short-ranged Jupiters from Turkey.

It is instructive that in his memoir, LeMay said nothing about the Cuban crisis. Published less than three years later, perhaps he felt constrained from writing due to security concerns. But more likely he was disgusted at the micromanagement exercised by McNamara and the timidity that LeMay perceived in the president. In LeMay's view, a rare opportunity to reverse Communist expansion had been squandered.

$\dashv\!\Longleftrightarrow\!\vdash$

In the spring of 1963 LeMay was appointed to a second term on the joint chiefs. It took everyone by surprise, including LeMay, who had expected to be retired "with a handshake and a few kind words." But in May President Kennedy asked the air force chief to remain for another year.[12]

There was precedent for the extension, as many service chiefs were retained for a total of three or even four years. However, Kennedy had already passed up Admiral George Anderson for renewal, as the navy chief had opposed administration defense policies nearly as much as LeMay. Almost certainly the reason for LeMay's retention was political: chopping two service chiefs in one year would focus attention on the discontent roiling around the JCS table, and LeMay had powerful friends in Congress. Some observers such as General McKee believed that Kennedy and McNamara were unwilling to expend political capital to replace LeMay.

Despite the often bitter interservice battles for roles and missions (to say nothing of appropriations) most of the service chiefs recognized the need for some accord among the various branches. That was, after all, one of the core reasons for establishing a unified defense department.

But there was also political horse trading to be done. Despite the XB-70 Valkyrie's perennial delays, LeMay was eager to see the high-tech bomber fully funded, and was willing to support a new aircraft carrier in exchange for navy endorsement of the Valkyrie. Thus was born CV-67, the yet unnamed ship that would become the last non-nuclear-powered carrier. Congress approved construction of the flat-top in 1963, with the keel laid in October 1964. By then the carrier's name had already been decided: USS *John F. Kennedy.*

But the bomber was already on the chopping block. In 1961 McNamara reduced the XB-70 program to three aircraft, then two "technology demonstrators." In January 1964 LeMay accepted the decision to build two Valkyries. It was a fiscal necessity in order to avert loss of the entire program budget of $1.5 billion, as the air force still could make use of the funding.

The first XB-70 was completed that summer but fuel system modifications kept it grounded until September, beginning a period as highspeed research aircraft. The second plane finally flew in 1965 and was destroyed in a midair collision in June 1966. In 1969 the surviving Valkyrie—evidence of Curtis LeMay's ultimate vision—was retired to the Air Force Museum in Ohio.

The summer of 1963 brought continued crisis in Southeast Asia as Buddhist dissidents resisted the Diem regime in Saigon while Communist guerrillas increased their activities against South Vietnam, Laos, and Cambodia. The U.S. Military Assistance Command in Saigon succeeded in keeping the lid on the unrest until August when *The New York Times* broke a story describing increased American involvement over the previous two years.

The administration reacted testily, the State Department denying that guerrilla attacks were increasing—which in fact they were. It is possible that the Washington view was skewed by optimistic reports from the field, but in any case the joint chiefs were heartily displeased with the situation. In large part, they felt shut off from the entire process.

From 1961 to 1963 Kennedy's top nineteen advisers on Vietnam (in Washington and Saigon) included only four military officers. The others were eight State Department officials, two intelligence specialists, and various cabinet or political figures.[13]

November 1963 was a watershed month. On November 2, South Vietnamese President Diem was killed in a military coup. It is uncertain that Kennedy knew of the plot, but the administration definitely was aware of it, including Saigon ambassador Henry Cabot Lodge.

The coup caught LeMay by surprise, though twenty years later he was convinced that the plotters had American help. In any case, he perceived an opportunity in the wake of Diem's death. He pointed out a constant in South Vietnamese politics: The military remained loyal to the government in power if for no other reason than self-interest. Consequently, a new opportunity had arisen to change American policy in Southeast Asia. LeMay never advocated large-scale commitment of U.S. ground troops to the region, but he believed that a stable Saigon government could eventually conquer the north beneath an umbrella of American airpower. He saw a direct relationship in Vietnam: Communist aggression from the north kept the south unstable, ergo the way to settle the region was to occupy the north.

The joint chiefs discussed their options for three more weeks. Then, on November 23, Kennedy was assassinated in Texas. LeMay was vacationing in Michigan that Friday but hastened back to Washington. On Sunday he was waiting in the White House to pay his respects to Jackie Kennedy, watching coverage of events in Dallas. Abruptly, accused assassin Lee Harvey Oswald was shot to death on live television. LeMay, who had dispassionately witnessed great cities reduced to ashes on his orders, was nevertheless astonished by the sudden violence. Joint Chiefs chairman Maxwell Taylor and some other military leaders expressed concern about a larger plot against the government, but LeMay dismissed the idea.

On November 29 President Lyndon Johnson met with the joint chiefs, stating that he would keep the same cabinet, which meant he was increasingly reliant upon McNamara and Taylor. From the war fighters' perspective, two worse choices could hardly have been made.

For the moment, LeMay was generally satisfied with the state of the air force, though experience would prove that it was top heavy at the strategic level and occasionally poorly prepared at the tactical level. But budget battles loomed large on the political horizon: Johnson was keenly aware that he would face an election in twelve months and he wanted to keep spending down. LeMay grumbled to himself, noting that America was spending more on fleet defense than on the North American Air Defense Command.

Another shift occurred just before year's end when Marine Corps Commandant David Shoup retired after four years on the JCS. He was succeeded by General Wallace M. Greene, who became LeMay's staunchest ally against administration defense policies.

Nuclear proliferation was a major concern in 1964 as China became the latest member of the atomic club, joining the United States, Russia, Britain, and France. But in June, Washington and Moscow completed the "hotline" agreement enabling emergency phone contact between the two capitols. Two months later came the limited test ban treaty.

That spring Lyndon Johnson asked LeMay about his retirement plans, seeking his recommendation for a successor. LeMay knew better than that: Anyone he recommended would almost certainly be axed by McNamara, so the chief merely said there were a dozen qualified officers. Johnson then astonished LeMay by offering him an ambassadorship, which he politely declined.

A few days later came another surprise. The president decided to retain his argumentative general by extending LeMay's tenure for another year. Johnson certainly knew of McNamara's contempt for LeMay, but the Texan was nothing if not politically astute. Undoubtedly he wanted to keep LeMay on a short leash during an election year, and General LeMay would not voice the professional military's low opinion of the D.C. crowd, as citizen LeMay surely would.

In July, army General Earle Wheeler became chairman of the joint chiefs and LeMay soon got a new vice chief. General John P. McConnell was well known to LeMay, having commanded the Second and Third Air Forces as well as directing SAC plans. However, he was a highly political general, personally friendly with Johnson and obedient to McNamara's wishes. It is unlikely that LeMay had a chance to endorse him, but in any case McConnell's choice meant that a compliant commander would lead the air force for the first four years of the Vietnam War.

<hr/>

Vietnam: If any year defined the course of the war, it was 1964.

When it came to drafting policy for Southeast Asia, Lyndon Baines Johnson believed in "four-letter words and short sentences." Furthermore, his advisors did not include the Joint Chiefs of Staff.

In March 1964 LeMay and Marine Corps Commandant Greene told LBJ that there were only two options in Vietnam: "either get in or get out." The Johnson administration did not welcome independent thinkers or truth tellers. Army chief George H. Decker had been forced out after two years for the heresy of stating that a conventional war could not be won in Southeast Asia.

Johnson's priorities were wholly political rather than geopolitical. It was nine long months to election day and he did not want to make Southeast Asia a campaign issue. Republicans such as Senator Barry Goldwater already were questioning the administration's stance against Communism.

In late May the JCS held a session while Maxwell Taylor prepared to accompany McNamara to a planning conference in Hawaii. LeMay chaired the meeting, which produced a memorandum expressing concern (it was in fact an indictment) over "a lack of definition, even a confusion in respect to objectives and courses of action" in Vietnam.[14]

Recognizing the ineffective measures thus far, the chiefs drafted a far more forceful policy to convince Hanoi to abandon its efforts to overthrow Saigon. Taylor refused to forward their proposal before leaving for Hawaii, nor did he present a modified version while there. He only presented it afterward, stating that he considered the service chiefs' perspective "inaccurate."[15]

Events escalated in August 1964 with two reports of North Vietnamese torpedo boats attacking American ships in the Tonkin Gulf. The first event actually occurred; the second was bogus. Nevertheless, the administration seized upon the second "incident" to demonstrate its resolve in resisting communist aggression. With Johnson's eyes focused on election day in November, retaliatory naval air strikes were launched against North Vietnam, beginning the longest bombing campaign in American history.

At the time of the Tonkin Gulf incidents, army General Earle Wheeler succeeded Taylor as chairman of the joint chiefs. Wheeler was the third consecutive army man appointed—a fact resented by the air force and navy since the top spot was supposed to rotate among the services.

After establishment of the Department of Defense in 1947, the first three chairmen followed an army-navy-air force sequence (Omar Bradley, Arthur Radford, and Nathan Twining). Thus, the second army chief, Lyman Lemnitzer, should have been succeeded by an admiral, and another airman. But Kennedy chose the army's Taylor and Wheeler, preventing another air force man from chairing until George Brown in 1974.

By rights, LeMay should have become chairman instead of Wheeler in July 1964. However, at that point LeMay was only seven months from retirement, and he would have required an exemption to extend his tenure into an unprecedented third term. Given his icy relations with the Johnson administration, the chances were less than zero.

Following Wheeler as the army's top soldier was Harold K. Johnson. Wheeler was an academic: a West Point mathematics instructor who spent most of World War II training National Guard units. However, he had excellent Washington contacts due to successive tours in D.C. In marked contrast, Harold Johnson had spent most of the war starving in Japanese prison camps but made an excellent combat record in Korea.

As summer turned to fall, it was clear to the joint chiefs that Lyndon Johnson and Robert McNamara were far more concerned with domestic political affairs than with Southeast Asia. The administration opted for the middle road, maintaining moderate air and naval pressure on North Vietnam while avoiding more effective—and more costly—measures advocated by LeMay and Greene. The airman and the marine favored sustained, powerful air strikes rather than the gradualist approach being pursued. As long as North Vietnam was immune from invasion, airpower represented the only option for keeping some pressure on Hanoi.[16]

Meanwhile, their adversary Maxwell Taylor was beginning to come around. He had been named ambassador to Saigon, where he witnessed the deteriorating situation firsthand. He began sending discrete reports to Washington, noting that LBJ's policy was failing.

At year end another program failure returned to haunt LeMay: the TFX tactical fighter that he had opposed as vice chief nearly four years previously. But in December 1964 the first prototype F-111A lifted off the General Dynamics' Texas runway, and the air force was well on the path to acquiring the controversial jet. However, despite its initial success, the swing-wing fighter soon hit a major snag: 40 percent cost overruns, raising unit cost from $4.5 to $6.3 million. LeMay's skepticism of the "Flying Edsel" had not been erased, even though the FB-111 became a SAC asset.

+>——<+

On a cold, blustery February day in 1965, Curtis LeMay ended his thirty-six-year military career. His first stop was the White House, where Lyndon Johnson bestowed the Distinguished Service Medal, a noncombat decoration that probably meant little to the recipient. By then LeMay already wore nine American combat decorations (Distinguished Service Cross, Silver Star, three Distinguished Flying Crosses, and four Air Medals) plus the usual "I-was-there" ribbons. He also had received combat awards from Britain, France, and Belgium. LeMay's critics would be surprised at three awards: the Medal for Humane Action (overseeing the Berlin Airlift) plus one each from the Soviet Union (1945) and Japan (1964). He was also recognized by seven other nations: Argentina, Brazil, Chile, Ecuador, Uruguay, Morocco, and Sweden.

In the formal retirement ceremony at Andrews Air Force Base, LeMay was surrounded by well wishers. Robert S. McNamara, who claimed illness, did not attend.

After the ceremony, the crowd of some 1,400 was treated to a flyover by airplanes significant to LeMay's career. Amid the jet bombers, tankers, fighters, and the Thunderbirds flight demonstration team was one relic that actually touched the old airman's heart. A restored B-17 had been summoned for the occasion, complete with the triangle G on the tail signifying the 305th Bomb Group.

LeMay turned over to his vice chief, John P. McConnell, whom he liked personally, but who proved a major disappointment to many air force officers. Already a drinking partner of Johnson's, he eagerly sided with LBJ and McNamara on policy matters. Whether due to alcoholic bonhomie or professional sycophancy, his priorities clearly were not with his aircrews flying and bleeding in Asian skies.

Be it irony or merely a sign of changing times, the contrast between LeMay's World War II service and his brief Vietnam tenure was vast. His authority as four-star air force chief of staff produced almost no influence in conduct of the Southeast Asian conflict, whereas he proved crucial in his two-star rank twenty years before.

The world had changed dramatically in two decades: so had America and the U.S. Air Force. Curtis Emerson LeMay had not.

CHAPTER TEN

Retirement

LEMAY HAD SWORN THAT ONE THING HE WOULD NOT DO IN retirement was write a book. Nevertheless, a memoir, *Mission with LeMay*, was published eight months later. It was written in much the manner he spoke: terse, choppy, pointed. Small wonder. Its coauthor, MacKinlay Kantor, was an old, trusted friend whom LeMay had known for more than twenty years, dating from the correspondent's wartime work in England. Kantor, a 1956 Pulitzer Prize winner, also had provided helpful coverage of the early days of SAC, and LeMay had enjoyed some the author's histories.

In his book, LeMay had little to say about his joint chief colleagues. For instance, he only mentioned Maxwell Taylor once, and then in passing. In contrast, after army General Harold Johnson retired in 1968, he described the Pentagon's civilian leadership as "intellectual prostitutes."[1]

The foreword to *Mission with LeMay* begins, "It could be that I have put my name to some inaccuracies in this book. I tried not to."

In that brief passage, LeMay unknowingly referenced his most-quoted sentiment. Apparently he accepted much of *Mission's* text at face value, with a cursory scan that left portions unedited. That lapse turned on him with a vengeance, as Kantor inserted a reference to bombing North Vietnam into the stone age—an attitude that LeMay never publicly expressed and that biographer Coffey implies he missed in proofreading. In any case, the fact that LeMay never recanted it opened him to cult status as a "caveman in a bomber."

The irony is that probably few of the people who vilified LeMay for his "stone age" sentiment toward North Vietnam would have thought twice had it been directed against Imperial Japan, let alone Nazi Germany. But the America of World War II was long gone by the 1960s, and drifting farther astern every year.

＋＞－－＜＋

The LeMays remained in the D.C. area for several months before deciding to move to California. The former chief of staff had received a lucrative offer from a new firm, Network Electronics, near Santa Monica. Part of the appeal, beyond a notable absence of sixteen-hour days, was the fact that Network had no government contracts. LeMay did not want to trade on his Pentagon contacts, so the concept pleased him. However, over the next two years relations soured with the company's owner, and LeMay left in 1968.

To the surprise of some, LeMay continued writing and thereby maintained a public presence. In his 1968 tome, *America Is in Danger,* he advocated maintaining a first-strike posture. He said, in part, "Deterrence cannot be assured in a no-win vacuum. It must rest not in the ability to withstand a first strike and retaliate effectively, but on the ability to launch a first strike and win if necessary." He further noted that overwhelming American nuclear superiority—with the ability to eviscerate the Soviet Union in a first blow—gave Kennedy the upper hand in Cuba.[2]

Were he living today (he would be one hundred in 2006), LeMay's world view would require considerable adjustment. The Soviet Union is defunct, SAC no longer exists, and Communism is limited to China, North Korea, Vietnam, and Cuba. Now, with America engaged in a long-term, low-intensity conflict, the doctrine of massive retaliation simply does not apply as it did in the twentieth century. When America was attacked in 2001, there were no readily identifiable targets to strike, let alone with thermonuclear bombers and missiles. Instead, the response took shape in small special forces teams inserted into Afghanistan, and later conventional forces committed to Iraq.

However, Curt LeMay might assert that America was attacked because her new enemies did not fear her. Whether retaliation for 9–11 came in the form of elite forces operating inside Taliban territory or "overkill" from a 500-pound bomb dropped on one *mujahadeen* guerrilla, the certainty of an American response lacks the deterrent effect of mutually assured destruction. Whatever else may be said of them, the ambitious realists in the Kremlin always could be counted upon to act in behalf of their own survival. That cannot be said of al Qaeda operatives, who glimpse paradise in the ephemeral glow of a suicide bomb.

Curtis LeMay was made for the twentieth century; he probably would not have enjoyed living in the twenty-first.

+>——<+

In 1967 LeMay was approached by influential California Republicans about running for the U.S. Senate. The next year would prove pivotal with the presidential election, but LeMay declined, at least in part because he felt uncomfortable as a fund raiser.

In 1968 LeMay was approached by Alabama governor George Wallace's American Independent Party (AIP), planning a major effort that fall. The AIP sought a running mate for Wallace, a conservative Democrat, but LeMay saw no future in third-party politics and turned down the AIP offer not once but twice, partly because he was suspicious of Wallace's racist background. Furthermore, LeMay believed that Republican Richard Nixon would reverse the disastrous Johnson foreign policy and generally turn the nation onto the conservative path he preferred. Therefore, LeMay did not want to detract from Nixon's base.[3]

Having been elected governor of Alabama in 1962, Wallace persisted. He had lost a previous bid partly because many Southern Democrats perceived him as too moderate, and reportedly he vowed never again "to be outniggered" by more overtly racist members of his party.[4]

Wallace's most quoted slogan—"Segregation now, segregation tomorrow, segregation forever"—was penned by a speechwriter for the new governor's inauguration. Though Wallace reportedly said that he had not read the speech before delivery, he could not recant the statement and retain credibility with his political base. That may have accounted for his actions a year later when he physically blocked access of two negro students to the University of Alabama. He finally stepped aside when confronted by federal marshals and national guardsmen.

However, as the campaign wore on, LeMay became increasingly concerned about Nixon's conservative credentials. Among other things, the GOP front runner relied upon moderate, "vanilla-flavored" Republicans such as New York's Nelson Rockefeller and Michigan's George Romney. Entering the party's convention that summer, Nixon appeared to have made so many deals to ensure early selection that he no longer appealed to LeMay. The California general called the Alabama governor and suggested a meeting.

LeMay's analysis proved accurate. Nixon, raised a Quaker, was no hard liner. He sought accommodation with the Soviets, and for Vietnam he proposed a phased withdrawal, described during the campaign as a "secret plan" to end American involvement, if not the war. Perhaps most galling of all to LeMay, Nixon retained Johnson's bombing halt of North Vietnam for three and a half years. Domestically, Nixon instituted wage and price controls that did not sit well with conservatives.

LeMay's first concern was to determine whether Wallace remained the stolid segregationist that he first appeared. After meeting with him, and satisfied that the Alabaman had moderated his views, LeMay agreed to run on the AIP ticket. The announcement came at nearly the last minute, on October 3, only four weeks before election day.[5]

Despite their similar outlooks, Wallace and LeMay formed a peculiar team, partly because Wallace was thirteen years younger than his running mate. An attorney and erstwhile boxer, he had joined the army air force in World War II and served in Brigadier General Roger Ramey's Fifty-eighth Bomb Wing, flying missions over Japan. The irony could not have been lost on LeMay; the junior officer who perennially surpassed his seniors suddenly found himself number two on the ticket to a former staff sergeant.

LeMay's decision to run on the American Independent ticket proved catastrophic to his reputation. Never a favorite of the tweedy Washington set in the first place, his alliance with Wallace sealed the allegation that he was, and had always been, a racist. That was demonstrably untrue: In 1950 he had integrated SAC without any problems when, in fact, the air force and the military generally led the nation in race relations. (Armed forces desegregation had begun in 1949, well ahead of the civilian sector.) Much of the criticism aimed at LeMay undoubtedly was disingenuous on that score, but there was no reversing the image. He was cast more than ever as the caveman in a bomber, and a bigoted caveman to boot.

In truth, LeMay probably gave very little thought to the race issue. He was far more concerned with defense matters, especially during the decade-long nightmare that was Vietnam. He viewed the prospect of a Democrat victory in 1968 as intolerable, especially since the party's nominee, Hubert Humphrey, was Johnson's vice president.

Humphrey was unlikely to have continued Johnson's failed policies, but the Minnesotan either could not or would not publicly disassociate himself from the administration. Consequently, he alienated many antiwar Democrats and independents, especially the young, who harassed Humphrey campaign appearances with cries of "Dump the hump!"

The curious couple on the American Independent ticket drew immediate attention. Caricatures of Wallace and LeMay were featured on the cover of *Time* magazine's October 18 issue, twenty-three years after LeMay's first appearance there.

Whatever the public perception, LeMay's rationale for running with Wallace remains perplexing. In any case, his logic was badly skewed. He stated that he ran with Wallace to prevent a Humphrey victory when clearly the Wallace candidacy posed no threat to the Democrats. The only thing that LeMay's participation could have done was to give Humphrey a narrow win by siphoning votes from the "hard hats," blue-collar, traditionally patriotic voters. In the end, Wallace and LeMay only succeeded in making Richard Nixon a plurality president. The American Independent Party won five states in the deep South, polling nearly ten million votes or 13 percent of the total, leaving Nixon-Agnew with 43 percent. Even then, it was a close-run campaign: Nixon only won by half a million votes from 73,000,000 cast.

In barely one month of campaigning, Wallace and LeMay nearly overturned one of the most important elections in American history.

LeMay had little contact with Wallace after the election, though the Alabaman remained in the political spotlight. Running again in 1972, Wallace was crippled by an assassin's bullets but recovered to resume his governorship. It was his second brush with death—he had nearly died in the army in 1945—leading to a religious conversion. Subsequently he fully recanted his previous segregationist views, completed his final term in 1987, and died near the state capitol eleven years later.

$$\cdot\!\!\!\longmapsto\!\!\!\longleftarrow\!\!\!\cdot$$

After the election, LeMay returned to activities and organizations that afforded most interest to him, including the National Geographic board of trustees, a position he had obtained in the 1950s.

LeMay remained in the public eye, receiving honorary doctor of laws degrees from John Carroll University, Kenyon College, the University of Southern California, Creighton University, and the University of Akron. He also held honorary doctor of science degrees from Tufts, Ohio State University, and the University of Virginia, and an honorary doctor of engineering degree from Case Institute of Technology.

However, the string of honors and recognition did not go to LeMay's head. He was far more interested in active projects that yielded tangible results, especially on behalf of airmen and their families. In 1964 LeMay and other aviation notables founded the Air Force Village Foundation, providing long-term residences for air force widows. The first two villages were built near San Antonio in the 1970s with others to follow.

Eventually the LeMays settled at the Air Force Village West near March Air Force Base at Riverside, California. Continuing to build on the village success, in 1987 they established the General and Mrs. Curtis E. LeMay Foundation to provide financial assistance to widows and widowers of air force retirees, regardless of rank.

Curtis Emerson LeMay—"the cold war's fiercest warrior"—died of heart failure at March Air Force Base on October 1, 1990, six weeks short of his eighty-fourth birthday. He was buried at the Air Force Academy, where his grave marker bears command pilot wings and the fact that he was a veteran of the Second World War. Almost as an after thought is inscribed, "Chief of Staff Jul 1961 Feb 1965."

CHAPTER 11

Debrief

HISTORIANS SOMETIMES PONDER THE CONCEPT OF THE irreplaceable leader. For obvious reasons, for good or ill, such men are rare: individuals the like of Caesar and Hannibal; Washington and Napoleon; Churchill and Hitler.

In the war against Japan, America may have possessed only two such commanders: An admiral and an airman. Their names were Chester Wilhelm Nimitz and Curtis Emerson LeMay.

General Douglas MacArthur certainly played a significant role, but he was not irreplaceable. Given the growing disparity of forces from 1943 onward, any competent general could have done what MacArthur did. The same might be said of Dwight Eisenhower in Europe.

Other "irreplaceable" contenders come to mind, largely from industry: Shipbuilders Henry Kaiser and Andrew Higgins; wingsmiths at Boeing, Douglas, Grumman; and North American physicist Robert Oppenheimer.

Whatever other names arise, Nimitz and LeMay were the two commanders most responsible for defeating the Japanese Empire. From 1942 through 1945, Nimitz had overall command of every significant Allied naval operation of the Pacific War, including the landmark battles from Midway to Okinawa. Bouncing back from the Pearl Harbor debacle, he proved the right man in the right place at the right time. In turn, his immediate subordinate, Fifth Fleet's Admiral Raymond A. Spruance, delivered the Marianas to XXI Bomber Command.

Though operating two echelons below Nimitz, the theater commander, LeMay was charged with waging war directly against the Japanese home islands. Even without the atomic bomb, he wielded power unprecedented in history. As General Lauris Norstad said, LeMay was the definitive operator: He knew his profession literally from the ground up, and he seldom if ever allowed his ego to interfere with results. He not only accepted the counsel of subordinates, but he worked as an ally with the army's perennial "enemy"—the U.S. Navy—in diverting B-29s to support the Okinawa landings, and in the immensely successful aerial mining campaign.

Certainly LeMay never claimed credit as the airman who brought Tokyo to its knees. He would have acknowledged the contribution of the naval aviators and the amphibious troops who gave him his Marianas bases, and the submariners who sank Japan's merchant marine. But had LeMay failed to produce the results that Arnold demanded of the B-29, most likely the invasion of Japan would have proceeded as the bloodiest battle in history. Though the estimate of 500,000 American dead certainly was excessive, Operation Downfall still had the potential to double the number of U.S. casualties in the Second World War.

Since 1945 the question has been debated with bitter conviction on both sides: Would Japan have surrendered without the B-29 campaign and the two A-bombs? Norstad felt that Tokyo would have capitulated without Hiroshima and Nagasaki; Eisenhower reportedly stated that Japan was trying to surrender "with a minim loss of face."[1]

Eisenhower erred. Even after Hiroshima, the Tokyo cabinet's response to the Potsdam Declaration remained intransigent. Japan communicated its "acceptance" via neutral channels: The emperor would retain all his powers, and behind the throne the military wanted no Allied occupation while the Japanese government would try its own war criminals. One can only conclude that Ike was woefully misinformed.

In May 1945, in an astonishing admission of gross naiveté, former President Hoover told Harry Truman, "I am convinced that if you . . . will make a shortwave broadcast to the people of Japan—tell them they can have their emperor if they surrender, that it will not mean unconditional surrender except for the militarists—you'll get a peace in Japan—you'll have both wars over."[2]

Hoover, no stranger to international politics, was somehow convinced that Japan was a democracy, guided by the will of the people.

Obviously the responsibility lay elsewhere. In any but the most despotic governments, LeMay's Tokyo fire raid of March 9–10, 1945 would have convinced the war cabinet to yield. The stench of a burning city and 80,000 corpses could not have gone unnoticed, yet the Bushido-driven rulers refused to surrender. Japanese cities were being dismantled on a nightly basis but national honor demanded a glorious national death. It had been no different amid the bomb-shattered rubble of Berlin three months before; in Hitler's view the Germans had lost his war so they deserved death and defeat.

It took Nagasaki and a Soviet declaration of war against Japan to convince Emperor Hirohito to override his zealous warlords.

Those who advocated a prolonged siege of Japan are often among LeMay's critics. The case is advanced that a months-long naval blockade would finally have compelled Tokyo to surrender, and that may be true. Food riots had erupted in May 1945 as bombing, mining, and submarine attacks choked off essential imports. Meanwhile, between 100,000 and 250,000 Asians were dying of starvation, disease, and Japanese brutality—every month.[3]

＋＞＝＜＋

Despite his austere, even severe public persona, LeMay was warmly regarded by those who knew him best. Colleagues described him as having "a heart of gold" and a "great feeling for the troops." But those same admirers quickly admitted that LeMay had no patience even for the well-intentioned nonperformers. "He'd fire you in a heartbeat," said one officer. Yet in contrast to his cultivated "tough guy" image, he built his own color television and played the organ.[4]

The seeming contradiction may be explained by LeMay's apparent ability to compartmentalize his personal and professional lives. Off duty, as an adult he enjoyed puttering and tinkering as much as he had in his youth. Yet the next day, back on duty, he was deadly serious, totally focused on the mission. In that regard, LeMay was much like a policeman who works in a violent world, seeing the worst of human behavior, but leaves his work at the door when he returns home. Other humans may only speculate upon the general's ability to plan for the incineration of millions of human beings, then spend a diverting few hours in his workshop before dinner.

Throughout his career, LeMay's preferred style was to lead his men from the front. Therefore, as a military commander it is ironic that he saw so little of his battlefield. Whether leading a bomb group or an air division, his view was necessarily limited to the head of the column, relying on tail gunners for information on what was happening astern. His view downward was restricted by the floor of his cockpit and, all too often, by clouds and flak barrages. Therefore, it is probable that in the twentieth century Curtis LeMay saw less of his combat arena than Ulysses Grant saw eighty years before. However, as an air force commander in China and the Marianas, the all-seeing eye of aerial reconnaissance laid bare the enemy homeland, allowing him to select targets and assess damage. It was the ultimate irony: The consummate air leader saw more and knew more from his headquarters than he or his crews did over the target.

Today, LeMay would laud the developments that provide an Argus-eyed view of the world through satellites and other sensors. To an extent, the awesome amount of imagery and information available to military commanders was initiated during his postwar tenure as chief of air force research and development. But it is less certain that the SAC general of the 1950s would welcome the degree of micromanagement that technology permits for twenty-first century politicians and administrators.

⊰══⊱

Most military leaders make some reference to looking out for their people; far fewer support words with actions. LeMay consistently proved that he meant what he said with improved housing, spot promotions, and a general atmosphere of supporting his subordinates. One example will suffice.

At Carswell Air Force Base in the 1950s LeMay arrived on board a commercial airliner declaring an "emergency." It was the start of a surprise operational readiness inspection, the dreaded ORI. Somehow the base commander had learned of the impending visit and went out of his way to present a spic and span image. He even assigned electronic technicians to scrub oil stains off the tarmac.

When LeMay descended from the DC-3, he looked around and commented on the unusually clean appearance of the flight line. The base commander, pleased at his coup, offered to show the commander in chief the rest of the facilities.

Then LeMay noticed the men wielding brooms. One of the sweepers was Airman Sam Korth, a radar specialist who had never seen a general before—let alone *the* general. He returned LeMay's gaze.

LeMay spun on a heel, glared at the base commander, and said, "Colonel, if your men have nothing better to do than this, then we don't need you. I'm instituting procedures to have you dismissed from the service. Get off my base."

Some thirty years later, Sam Korth met LeMay at an air show and asked if the popular story was true: Allegedly LeMay had smoked a cigar while standing under a B-36 and was warned that the Peacemaker might explode. Reportedly the general had responded, "It wouldn't dare."

LeMay grunted, then said, "I started that story. But I always followed my own orders."

Korth was able to pose with his former commander and even managed to place an arm on the great man's shoulder, adding, "I couldn't bring myself to call him 'Curt' but I cannot begin to say how much I respected him as a leader."[5]

+===+

Two of the world's greatest airmen of LeMay's generation were Jimmy Doolittle and Charles Lindbergh. All were leaders and extremely proficient technicians: Doolittle gained one of the earliest aeronautics Ph.D.s and was one of the finest stick-and-rudder men of his lifetime. He was accurately called "a master of the calculated risk."

That same assessment applied to Lindbergh, who rolled destiny's golden dice and won the biggest pot of all. By flying solo from New York to Paris, he redefined the limits of glory. In the tawdry era of gin-soaked cynicism called Prohibition, he remained the ultimate aesthete: above the crowd that clamored for him.

Unlike Doolittle and LeMay, Lindbergh evolved from an early worshiper of "scientific materialism" into a technical heretic. He wrote, "I have seen the science I worshiped, and the aircraft I loved, destroying the civilization I expected them to serve."[6]

Doolittle was not without a spiritual aspect. In comparing bomber pilots and fighter pilots, he said, "A fighter pilot is alone in his aeroplane, just he and his deity. A bomber pilot is part of a team that relies each upon the other." Then he grinned and concluded, "From a family with two generations of fighter pilots, I must confess that there has been little evolution in our line!"[7]

LeMay knew exactly what Doolittle meant. Whether in a B-17 over Europe, a B-29 over Japan, or a B-52 on the periphery of the Evil Empire, LeMay's professional life revolved around leadership, teamwork, and maximum efficiency.

Lindbergh was a risk taker; he was about self-control. Doolittle was an engineer; he was about precision.

Curt LeMay was, as Norstad said, an operator. He was about results.

Ira Eaker once described LeMay as a "today general," highly competent across the board but excelling in assessing current forces and employing them with maximum effectiveness.[8]

+>==+==<+

LeMay's public image hovers somewhere between marginal and disastrous. His appearance and behavior—inevitably described as gruff, jowly, and scowling—were not calculated to win admiration. Nor could they have, given the context. In the halcyon days of Camelot, when bright, attractive young leaders began replacing the drab, balding occupants of the White House, America seemed to reinvent its concept of leaders. In sequence, Truman walked; Eisenhower golfed; the Kennedys sailed.

Curt LeMay went hunting.

Intellectual writer Irving F. Stone popularized the notion of LeMay as a "caveman in a bomber." Beyond that, CinCSAC lent himself to the impression of a Strangelovian barbarian eager to conduct nuclear war with the Communist world. Presumably only the well-heeled, civilized aristocrats in Washington restrained the nuclear neanderthal from dragging his hairy knuckles across the apocalyptic button. It was as if SAC and indeed the cold war had been created in a geopolitical vacuum, absent the churning ambition spreading its totalitarian philosophy outward from the Eurasian landmass.

Certainly LeMay evidenced no concern for his public image. If he was perceived as a warmonger or a racist, he spent precious little time refuting either assertion. In that regard he appeared vastly indifferent to his historical status, yet seemingly he remained supremely self-composed. It was as if he had nothing to prove to anyone, least of all to himself.

The one exception would have been to his aircrews. Throughout his military career, LeMay proved time and again that he genuinely cared about the men who flew his airplanes, and those who kept them flying. While it might be tempting to attribute his demonstrated concern to an underlying sentimentality, the greater share of truth probably lies elsewhere. LeMay was an ultimate realist, and he knew that the best way to keep his people productive was to keep them well housed, well fed, and well led.

If such was the case, the formula worked for a period spanning decades: from Regensburg to Tokyo to Omaha—and even to Moscow. Everywhere, it seems, but Washington, D.C.

CHAPTER 12

The Legacy

IT IS NOT RECORDED THAT ANYONE EVER ACCUSED CURTIS LeMay of charisma. Perhaps no other American military leader of the twentieth century was consistently so successful without possessing a charismatic personality: Whether the avuncular quality of an Eisenhower or the flamboyance of a Patton. As often noted, LeMay's appearance and demeanor often kept even close associates at arm's length. Probably he wanted it that way, as he chose his friends with extreme care, evidently with the same precision of a preflight inspection of a new aircraft.

Consequently, LeMay's leadership lessons are more easily discerned than those of more intuitive, less clinical commanders. Yet the application of those factors can be no less daunting for leaders and managers seeking to emulate his success. After all, LeMay's apparently easy mastery of an enormously complex, constantly changing profession was only achieved after decades of experience.

LeMay's military philosophy has been well documented: Overwhelming force unstintingly applied until the enemy capitulates. He recognized that the Clauswitzian principle of mass coupled with twentieth century technology produced not only victory, but (in the nuclear era) even more importantly, it produced deterrence.

However, following his record tenure as CinCSAC, LeMay's influence waned considerably. After the Korean armistice he seems to have assumed that the folly of waging a limited land war in Asia would never recur, and consequently he remained focused upon the strategic mission. In part due to his perception, the air force entered Vietnam barely a decade later, marginally prepared to conduct a large-scale tactical war. In that regard, LeMay misread not only the likely enemy, but the dramatic shift in America's political leadership.

During his time on the Joint Chiefs, LeMay experienced little more than frustration. He was confident of the advice he offered—avoid another Asian land war by massive application of airpower—but his professional opinion went not merely unheeded: It was unwelcome by the civilian leadership. By the time he realized that the JCS assessment of Southeast Asia was alternately being misrepresented and ignored within the Johnson administration, he was months from retirement.

Had LeMay been eligible to remain on the Joint Chiefs into 1966 or 1967, perhaps the Pentagon pot would have reached a boil. Almost certainly he would not have allowed the escalation of North Vietnam's air defenses as did his successor, General McConnell: Permitting missile sites to be completed before they were attacked, and prohibiting strikes on MiG fields. Under those conditions, it is possible that LeMay would have resigned in protest and carried his message to the public, as he did in 1968.

Had he done so, LeMay would have been in rare company. Since World War II, only two service chiefs have resigned over matters of policy with which they disagreed. Ironically, perhaps, the first was Admiral Louis Denfeld, who protested the Truman administration's cancellation of a new-generation aircraft carrier during the B-36 controversy. The second was an airman, General Ronald Fogelman, who protested the treatment of a subordinate blamed for casualties in a terrorist bombing in Arabia. Whatever reservations other JCS members have held about defense policy over the past six decades, none have felt strongly enough to lay their stars on the table.

⊬⊣⊢⊦

In order to determine the factors behind LeMay's success as a leader, it is only necessary to examine his methods in World War II and in SAC. Briefly stated, his success was based on a few guiding principles:

1. Thoroughly mastering his craft. It was said that LeMay was the best pilot, best navigator, and best bombardier in every unit he served. That may be something of an exaggeration, but it's consistent enough to bear examination. Already an accomplished pilot in 1937, he cross-trained himself in navigation and bombing to achieve complete familiarity with the essential tasks of his trade. Having proved the concept personally, then he applied it to his aircrews.
2. Leading by example. LeMay was an up-front leader: He demonstrated not only exceptional competence, but a consistent willingness to share the risk with his troops. The two best examples were the Regensburg attack, when he was a wing leader not expected to fly the "rough ones," and the B-29 mission he managed over Manchuria. Nevertheless, he was seldom if ever a micromanager. As long as his subordinates produced results, usually he left them alone.
3. Providing accountability. LeMay rewarded success and punished failure. Accountability lay at the core of the spot

promotion concept: It recognized superior performance and told the "troops" that their efforts were appreciated. At times he seemed severe in his judgments, but in context of nuclear deterrence, he could not afford to distinguish between the incompetent and the unlucky.

4. Identifying and producing subordinate leaders. LeMay's immensely successful "lead crew" program dramatically improved combat performance in Europe and the Pacific. He then applied it to SAC, where the idea paid double dividends: increased performance which, coupled with spot promotions, enhanced morale and therefore retention.

5. Communicating with his people. Throughout his career, LeMay made a point of telling his command what he expected, sometimes in clinical detail. He produced shelves of manuals describing how every function should be accomplished. However, if someone suggested a better way of doing things, he was consistently receptive.

6. Encouraging teamwork. Though originally a single-seat fighter pilot, LeMay's professional instincts pulled him in the other direction: bombardment aviation. Because a bomber crew is necessarily a team, so too is a bomb squadron, group, and wing. Therefore, LeMay not only recognized the obvious nature of the enterprise, but worked tirelessly to improve it. There is an internal logic to his approach. Teamwork was the product of technical mastery, communication and coordination, and leadership. Coupled with accountability, it was a self-sustaining approach that proved itself repeatedly under adverse circumstances: In the flak-filled skies of Europe and Asia, in sustaining a major city under siege, and throughout the coldest portion of the decades-long cold war.

LeMay's legacy to the air force has diminished with the service's changing missions, though the B-52 that he brought into service in

1956 remains an active icon half a century later, outliving SAC itself. The air force's cold war mission was deterrence. That situation changed with collapse of the Soviet Union in 1989–90. SAC stood down in 1992, its component units largely transferred to the new Air Combat Command.

Institutionally, the air force remained bomber oriented for years after LeMay's departure. His four successors were bomber pilots, a pattern that lasted through the 1970s.

Ironically, SAC fell into the hands of fighter pilots during the Vietnam War, and it was not for the best. At the height of the air war, Operation Linebacker II unleashed B-52s against North Vietnam in late 1972, seeking to restart the stalled peace negotiations. CinCSAC was General John C. Meyer, a quadruple ace with Messerschmitts and MiGs to his credit and a personality almost as dour as LeMay. His subordinate commanders at the Seventh and Eighth Air Forces also were World War II aces. Among them, they conducted a combing campaign notably lacking in imagination: An almost airline routine with predictable altitudes, routes, and schedules. Losses were serious: Fifteen Stratoforts shot down in less than two weeks, but the professionalism of the crews kept the bombs out on the hard targets, to the fervent cheers of fellow airmen who had languished for years in the Hanoi Hilton.

With signing of the Paris treats in January 1973, SAC helped win a notable political goal, as military victory was denied by two presidential administrations. But for years afterward, B-52 crews sipped their "suds" in officers' clubs happy hours and reflected that, whatever his faults, Curt LeMay would never have conducted such a poorly conceived campaign.

+>===<+

Among the changes ensuing from LeMay's retirement was greater use of Air National Guard assets. When his prejudice against the guard was no longer a factor, the way eventually was cleared for SAC to make use of tankers previously dedicated to Tactical Air Command (TAC). At that point a senior noncommissioned airman explained, "With the '135s we were finally 'SACumcized' and everyone was happy except TAC."[1]

For good or ill, the air force took years to outlive LeMay's imprint. Some SAC insiders felt that after LeMay, Offutt became a preretirement home for up-and-out generals who seldom wavered from LeMay's way of doing things. It was seen as a guaranteed place of rest for the last two years of their careers, where nobody was likely to spoil the easy ride.

In the view of many, not until General Russell Dougherty took over in 1974 was the LeMay influence finally put to rest. Dougherty considered himself "the first non-hero to command the Strategic Air Command." It was said of Dougherty, "He was the guy who finally made SAC part of the air force." Reportedly he called a meeting of his staff and said there was nothing in the regulations that required them to be SOBs, and things changed for the better.[2]

In a 1996 interview, Dougherty said, "I thought General LeMay was a brilliant man with magnificent military acumen. He was rejected out of hand often times. He's not an easy man to take. He's not personable and he's not a jokester. Neither was Mr. McNamara. So they had a very rough relationship."[3]

Not surprisingly, LeMay was most appreciated by his fellow airmen. While comparing notes with Jimmy Doolittle, Ira Eaker said that LeMay had been his best combat leader. Doolittle agreed, adding that having watched LeMay in Europe and the Pacific, he was likely "the best air commander the U.S. or any other nation ever produced."[4]

The doctrine of massive retaliation that LeMay advocated found itself overtaken by events. With no "peer opponent" on the horizon, the air force restructured itself to meet the needs of a changed geopolitical landscape. The futuristic, stealthy B-2, designed and purchased as the ultimate doomsday machine, became a pariah to many air force pilots. Despite a vastly reduced mission, it soaked up enormous sums that could have gone to acquisition of more useful aircraft plus spare parts and fuel.

The B-52 remains, but its importance diminished as the A-10 attack aircraft, C-5 transport, and HH-53 helicopter assumed more prominent positions at the tip of the spear. As of this writing, aerial combat has become a dim memory: From 1975 through 2005, air force fighters claimed merely forty-five shootdowns. Al Qaeda does not possess an air force (that's why the 9–11 terrorists seized American airplanes), and the next dogfight appears nowhere on the horizon. It is possible that the next ace has not been born—or that no more aces will ever be born.

The precision revolution also has changed the service in ways that Curtis LeMay probably did not envision. During World War II, Korea, and Vietnam, planners assigned large numbers of aircraft to each target. With the arrival of the technological millennium, targeters now assign multiple aim points to individual airplanes.

None of the foregoing is surprising. LeMay lived a richly varied career that spanned the period from open-cockpit biplanes to supersonic jets and nuclear weapons. Change was inevitable; it is intrinsic to aviation. But LeMay's enduring legacy is not technical: It is leadership. He inherited the examples of Billy Mitchell and Robert Olds, and passed them on to the next generation of airmen. As such, he represented the continuum of the U.S. Air Force as an enduring institution.

Perhaps LeMay's most instructive definition of leadership arose from a discussion with air force reserve officer applicants. He told them, "No matter how well you apply the art of leadership, no matter how strong your unit, or how high the morale of your men, if your leadership is not directed completely toward the mission, your leadership has failed." Pressed for a one-word definition of leadership, he paused momentarily, then said, "Responsibility."[5]

In those two replies, Curtis LeMay distilled the essence of his experience and philosophy. Results were measured by success, which perhaps is why his memoir was titled *Mission with LeMay*. The mission—attainment of the goal—was his professional holy grail. But it could not be achieved without responsibility. He accepted an increasing burden of responsibility throughout his career: navigating across thousands of miles; leading a green unit over Occupied Europe; commanding the world's greatest bomber fleet against Japan; feeding a city during the Berlin blockade; building America's primary deterrent literally from the ground up.

LeMay did not complete any of his missions by gentle persuasion. In the words of a subordinate, "Curt LeMay irritated many people, *but,* he usually ended up right. I wonder what would have happened if his superiors had listened to him about Vietnam."[6]

<hr/>

LeMay's controversial reputation raises the question of what it really means to be a "good soldier": Does he robotically execute policy he believes will fail, or does he exercise his judgment? Throughout his career, LeMay bluntly stated his professional opinion; if it was ignored, he refrained from speaking publicly as long as he wore the uniform. But once he hung up his "blue suit," he felt no constraints on expressing his misgivings and offering alternatives.

It has often been noted that LeMay was not a successful air force chief of staff. But that assertion begs the unasked question: in the 1960s, what service chief was "successful"? If LeMay was constantly at odds with the Johnson-McNamara cabal that consistently mismanaged America's most disastrous foreign war, that failed utterly in its obligation to the troops, what does that say of those who were "good soldiers," who for personal or parochial reasons pursued a fatally flawed policy?

Sometimes a soldier can do his nation no greater disservice than following orders.

<hr/>

For thirty years or more, many statements were attributed to LeMay, but perhaps one is most telling of all. Asked what he would do if nuclear war erupted, CinCSAC reportedly said that in such circumstances, he had failed in his deterrent mission and the only honorable thing left to do was man up a B-52 and launch for Moscow.

Whether he ever said it or not is irrelevant. The attitude was the essence of Curtis Emerson LeMay.

Notes

Chapter 1

1. Curtis E. LeMay with MacKinlay Kantor, *Mission with LeMay: My Story* (New York: Doubleday, 1965), 14.
2. Curtis E. LeMay with MacKinlay Kantor, *Mission with LeMay: My Story* (New York: Doubleday, 1965), 18.
3. Curtis E. LeMay with MacKinlay Kantor, *Mission with LeMay: My Story* (New York: Doubleday, 1965), 30.
4. Curtis E. LeMay with MacKinlay Kantor, *Mission with LeMay: My Story* (New York: Doubleday, 1965), 95.
5. Dik Alan Daso, *Hap Arnold and the Evolution of American Airpower* (Washington, D.C.: Smithsonian Institution Press, 2000), 132.
6. Curtis E. LeMay with MacKinlay Kantor, *Mission with LeMay: My Story* (New York: Doubleday, 1965), 111.
7. Curtis E. LeMay with MacKinlay Kantor, *Mission with LeMay: My Story* (New York: Doubleday, 1965), 114.

Chapter 2

1. Curtis E. LeMay with MacKinlay Kantor, *Mission with LeMay: My Story* (New York: Doubleday, 1965), 131.
2. Curtis E. LeMay with MacKinlay Kantor, *Mission with LeMay: My Story* (New York: Doubleday, 1965), 138.
3. Curtis E. LeMay with MacKinlay Kantor, *Mission with LeMay: My Story* (New York: Doubleday, 1965), 185.
4. Curtis E. LeMay with MacKinlay Kantor, *Mission with LeMay: My Story* (New York: Doubleday, 1965), 187.

5. Curtis E. LeMay with MacKinlay Kantor, *Mission with LeMay: My Story* (New York: Doubleday, 1965), 193.
6. Curtis E. LeMay with MacKinlay Kantor, *Mission with LeMay: My Story* (New York: Doubleday, 1965), 206.
7. Curtis E. LeMay with MacKinlay Kantor, *Mission with LeMay: My Story* (New York: Doubleday, 1965), 208
8. Curtis E. LeMay with MacKinlay Kantor, *Mission with LeMay: My Story* (New York: Doubleday, 1965), 208.

Chapter 3

1. Curtis E. LeMay with MacKinlay Kantor, *Mission with LeMay: My Story* (New York: Doubleday, 1965), 210.
2. Walter J. Boyne, "LeMay," *Air Force Magazine*, Vol. 81, No. 3, March 1998.
3. Curtis E. LeMay with MacKinlay Kantor, *Mission with LeMay: My Story* (New York: Doubleday, 1965), 217.
4. Curtis E. LeMay with MacKinlay Kantor, *Mission with LeMay: My Story* (New York: Doubleday, 1965), 230.
5. Curtis E. LeMay with MacKinlay Kantor, *Mission with LeMay: My Story* (New York: Doubleday, 1965), 231.
6. Thomas M. Coffey, *Iron Eagle: The Turbulent Life of General Curtis LeMay* (New York: Crown Publishers, 1986), 33.
7. Curtis E. LeMay with MacKinlay Kantor, *Mission with LeMay: My Story* (New York: Doubleday, 1965), 231.
8. Ronald H. Bailey, *World War II: The Air War in Europe* (Alexandria: Time-Life Books,1979), 81.
9. Thomas M. Coffey, *Iron Eagle: The Turbulent Life of General Curtis LeMay* (New York: Crown Publishers, 1986), 35.
10. Coffey, p. 38.
11. Thomas M. Coffey, *Iron Eagle: The Turbulent Life of General Curtis LeMay* (New York: Crown Publishers, 1986), 41.
12. Thomas M. Coffey, *Iron Eagle: The Turbulent Life of General Curtis LeMay* (New York: Crown Publishers, 1986), 48.
13. Curtis E. LeMay with MacKinlay Kantor, *Mission with LeMay: My Story* (New York: Doubleday, 1965), 285.
14. Curtis E. LeMay with MacKinlay Kantor, *Mission with LeMay: My Story* (New York: Doubleday, 1965), 286.
15. Curtis E. LeMay with MacKinlay Kantor, *Mission with LeMay: My Story* (New York: Doubleday, 1965), 357.
16. Thomas M. Coffey, *Iron Eagle: The Turbulent Life of General Curtis LeMay* (New York: Crown Publishers, 1986), 440.
17. Thomas M. Coffey, *Iron Eagle: The Turbulent Life of General Curtis LeMay* (New York: Crown Publishers, 1986), 18; and Curtis E. LeMay with MacKinlay Kantor, *Mission with LeMay: My Story* (New York: Doubleday, 1965), 288, 293.
18. Thomas M. Coffey, *Iron Eagle: The Turbulent Life of General Curtis LeMay* (New York: Crown Publishers, 1986), 88.

19. Curtis E. LeMay with MacKinlay Kantor, *Mission with LeMay: My Story* (New York: Doubleday, 1965), 303.
20. Curtis E. LeMay with MacKinlay Kantor, *Mission with LeMay: My Story* (New York: Doubleday, 1965), 314.

Chapter 4

1. Curtis E. LeMay with MacKinlay Kantor, *Mission with LeMay: My Story* (New York: Doubleday, 1965), 321–22.
2. Richard B. Frank, *Downfall: The End of the Japanese Empire* (New York, Random House, 1999), 57.
3. Richard B. Frank, *Downfall.* (New York, Random House, 1999), 55.
4. Thomas M. Coffey, *Iron Eagle: The Turbulent Life of General Curtis LeMay* (New York: Crown Publishers, 1986), 128.

Chapter 5

1. Herman Wolk, "Airman in the Shadows." *Air Force Magazine,* Vol. 88, No. 8, August 2005
2. Thomas M. Coffey, *Iron Eagle: The Turbulent Life of General Curtis LeMay* (New York: Crown Publishers, 1986), 132.
3. USAAF Statistical Summary of World War II.
4. Dik Alan Daso, *Hap Arnold and the Evolution of American Airpower* (Washington, D.C.: Smithsonian Institution Press, 2000), 207.
5. Ronald Schaffer, *Wings of Judgment: American Boming in World War II* (London: Oxford University Press, 1985), 126–27.
6. Curtis E. LeMay with MacKinlay Kantor, *Mission with LeMay: My Story* (New York: Doubleday, 1965), 353.
7. Richard B. Frank, *Downfall: The End of the Japanese Empire* (New York, Random House, 1999), 17.
8. *Fog of War,* dir. Errol Morris, 2003. Encore Drama channel; June 1, 2005.
9. Curtis E. LeMay with MacKinlay Kantor, *Mission with LeMay: My Story* (New York: Doubleday, 1965), 388.
10. Curtis E. LeMay with MacKinlay Kantor, *Mission with LeMay: My Story* (New York: Doubleday, 1965), 354.
11. Curtis E. LeMay with MacKinlay Kantor, *Mission with LeMay: My Story* (New York: Doubleday, 1965), 355.
12. Thomas M. Coffey, *Iron Eagle: The Turbulent Life of General Curtis LeMay* . (New York: Crown Publishers, 1986), 161.
13. Gordon Thomas and Max Morgan Wits, *The Enola Gay* (New York, Pocket Books, 1977), 183–4.
14. USAAF Statistical Summary of World War II.
15. Dik Alan Daso, *Hap Arnold and the Evolution of American Airpower* (Washington, D.C.: Smithsonian Institution Press, 2000), 207.
16. Ronald Schaffer, *Wings of Judgment: American Boming in World War II* (London: Oxford University Press, 1985), 130.

17. Curtis E. LeMay with MacKinlay Kantor, *Mission with LeMay: My Story* (New York: Doubleday, 1965), 375.

18. Curtis E. LeMay with MacKinlay Kantor, *Mission with LeMay: My Story* (New York: Doubleday, 1965), 387.

Chapter 6

1. Jeffrey G. Barlow, *Revolt of the Admirals: The Fight For Naval Aviation 1945–1950* (Washington D.C.: Naval History Center, 1994), 315.

2. Thomas M. Coffey, *Iron Eagle: The Turbulent Life of General Curtis LeMay* (New York: Crown Publishers, 1986), 249–250.

3. Jeffrey G. Barlow, *Revolt of the Admirals: The Fight For Naval Aviation 1945–1950* (Washington D.C.: Naval History Center, 1994), 76–77.

4. Jeffrey G. Barlow, *Revolt of the Admirals* (Washington D.C.: Naval History Center, 1994), 90.

5. Curtis E. LeMay with MacKinlay Kantor, *Mission with LeMay: My Story* (New York: Doubleday, 1965), 259.

6. Curtis E. LeMay with MacKinlay Kantor, *Mission with LeMay: My Story* (New York: Doubleday, 1965), 263.

Chapter 7

1. Jeffrey G. Barlow, *Revolt of the Admirals: The Fight For Naval Aviation 1945–1950* (Washington D.C.: Naval History Center, 1994), 101.

2. Curtis E. LeMay with MacKinlay Kantor, *Mission with LeMay: My Story* (New York: Doubleday, 1965), 482.

3. Jeffrey G. Barlow, *Revolt of the Admirals: The Fight For Naval Aviation 1945–1950.* (Washington D.C.: Naval History Center, 1994), 101–2.

4. Curtis E. LeMay with MacKinlay Kantor, *Mission with LeMay: My Story* (New York: Doubleday, 1965), 433.

5. Richard H. Kohn and Joseph P. Harahan. *Strategic Air Warfare* (Bolling Air Force Base: Office of Air Force History, 1988), 95.

6. Major T.J. Crowley. *Curtis E. LeMay: The Enduring Big Bomber Man* U.S. Marine Corps Command and Staff College, Quantico, Virginia, 1986.

7. Jeffrey G. Barlow, *Revolt of the Admirals: The Fight For Naval Aviation 1945–1950* (Washington D.C.: Naval History Center, 1994), 227.

8. Jeffrey G. Barlow, *Revolt of the Admirals: The Fight For Naval Aviation 1945–1950* (Washington D.C:. Naval History Center, 1994), 227.

9. Jeffrey G. Barlow, *Revolt of the Admirals* (Washington D.C.: Naval History Center, 1994), 230.

10. Natural Resources Defense Council, Table of USSR and Russian Nuclear Warheads, available at http://www.nrD.C..org/nuclear/nudb/datab10.asp

11. Major William H. Allen, USAF (Ret), email correspondence with author, November 24, 2005.

12. Major William H. Allen, USAF (Ret), email correspondence with author, November 24, 2005.

13. Major William H. Allen, USAF (Ret), email correspondence with author, November 24, 2005.

14. *Professional Pilot,* June 26, 1950.
15. Richard H. Kohn and Joseph P. Harahan, *Strategic Air Warfare* (Bolling Air Force Base: Office of Air Force History, 1988), 86–7.
16. Richard H. Kohn and Joseph P. Harahan, *Strategic Air Warfare* (Bolling Air Force Base: Office of Air Force History, 1988), 92.
17. Curtis E. LeMay with MacKinlay Kantor, *Mission with LeMay: My Story* (New York: Doubleday, 1965), 459.
18. Donald Quarles: "Lagging Research and Development." *Air Force Magazine,* January 1956, Vol. 39, No. 1.
19. William E. Burrows, *By Any Means Necessary: America's Secret Air War in the Cold War* (New York: Farrar, Straus, and Giroux, 2001), 60.
20. Richard H. Kohn and Joseph P. Harahan, *Strategic Air Warfare* (Bolling Air Force Base: Office of Air Force History, 1988), 108.
21. Richard H. Kohn and Joseph P. Harahan, *Strategic Air Warfare* (Bolling Air Force Base: Office of Air Force History, 1988), 109.

Chapter 8

1. William E. Burrows, *By Any Means Necessary: America's Secret Air War in the Cold War* (New York: Farrar, Straus, and Giroux, 2001), 353–356.
2. William E. Burrows, *By Any Means Necessary* (New York: Farrar, Straus, and Giroux, 2001), 184–87.
3. "U.S. Nuclear History," nsarchive.chadwyck.com/nh_essay.htm
4. "U.S. Nuclear History," nsarchive.chadwyck.com/nh_essay.htm.
5. Richard H. Kohn and Joseph P. Harahan. *Strategic Air Warfare* (Bolling Air Force Base: Office of Air Force History, 1988), 95–96.
6. Kohn, 98.
7. Kohn, 99.
8. Curtis E. LeMay with MacKinlay Kantor, *Mission with LeMay: My Story* (New York: Doubleday, 1965), 479
9. Ronald Schaffer, *Wings of Judgment: American Boming in World War II* (London: Oxford University Press, 1985), 203.
10. Curtis E. LeMay with MacKinlay Kantor, *Mission with LeMay: My Story* (New York: Doubleday, 1965), 473.
11. Richard H. Kohn and Joseph P. Harahan, *Strategic Air Warfare* (Bolling Air Force Base: Office of Air Force History, 1988), 101.
12. "On the Importance of Image: Some Lessons from the B-52." www.airpower. maxwell.af.mil/airchronicles/apj/apj94/baker.html#contributor
13. Thomas M. Coffey, *Iron Eagle: The Turbulent Life of General Curtis LeMay* (New York: Crown Publishers, 1986), 319.
14. Master Sergeant Ken Tomb (Ret.), email correspondence with author, October 2005.
15. "Bulletin of Atomic Scientists: Estimated U.S. and Soviet/Russian Nuclear Stockpiles." www.thebulletin.org/article_nn.php?art_ofn=nd94norris.
16. "Digital National Security Archive: U.S. Nuclear History 1955–1968." www. nsarchive.chadwyck.com/nh_essay.htm#54

Chapter 9

1. Curtis E. LeMay with MacKinlay Kantor, *Mission with LeMay: My Story* (New York: Doubleday, 1965), 347.
2. Captain Donald Gordon, USN (Ret.), December 1, 2005.
3. Walter.J. Boyne, "LeMay." *Air Force* Magazine, March 1998.
4. Thomas M. Coffey, *Iron Eagle: The Turbulent Life of General Curtis LeMay* (New York: Crown Publishers, 1986), 355.
5. Richard B. Frank, *Downfall: The End of the Japanese Empire* (New York, Random House, 1999), and *Fog of War,* Encore Drama Channel, June 1, 2005.
6. *Fog of War,* dir. Errol Morris, 2003. Encore Drama channel; June 1, 2005.
7. "Robert McNamara's Mutual Deterrence Speech." www.everything.blockstackers. com/index.pl?node_id=488842
8. Richard H. Kohn and Joseph P. Harahan, *Strategic Air Warfare* (Bolling Air Force Base: Office of Air Force History, 1988), 110.
9. Thomas M. Coffey, *Iron Eagle: The Turbulent Life of General Curtis LeMay* (New York: Crown Publishers, 1986), 390.
10. *Fog of War,* dir. Errol Morris, 2003. Encore Drama channel; June 1, 2005.
11. Thomas M. Coffey, *Iron Eagle: The Turbulent Life of General Curtis LeMay* (New York: Crown Publishers, 1986), 392.
12. Thomas M. Coffey, *Iron Eagle: The Turbulent Life of General Curtis LeMay* (New York: Crown Publishers, 1986), 424.
13. "John F. Kennedy and His Advisers." www.richmond.edu/~ebolt/history398/US-AdvisoryExperience(1954–1965).html
14. H.R. McMaster, *Dereliction of Duty: Lyndon Johnson, Robert McNamara, the Joint Chief of Staff, and the Lies that Led to Vietnam* (New York: Harper Perennial, 1997), 100.
15. H.R. McMaster, *Dereliction of Duty: Lyndon Johnson, Robert McNamara, the Joint Chief of Staff, and the Lies that Led to Vietnam* (New York: Harper Perennial, 1997, 101.
16. H.R. McMaster, *Dereliction of Duty: Lyndon Johnson, Robert McNamara, the Joint Chief of Staff, and the Lies that Led to Vietnam* (New York: Harper Perennial, 1997, 70.

Chapter 10

1. "General Harold K. Johnson." www.arlingtoncemetery.net/hkjohnson.htm
2. 2. William E. Burrows, *By Any Means Necessary: America's Secret Air War in the Cold War* (New York: Farrar, Straus, and Giroux, 2001), 60.
3. Thomas M. Coffey, *Iron Eagle: The Turbulent Life of General Curtis LeMay* (New York: Crown Publishers, 1986), 445.
4. "George C. Wallace" encyclopedia.thefreedictionary.com/George%20Wallace.
5. Thomas M. Coffey, *Iron Eagle: The Turbulent Life of General Curtis LeMay* (New York: Crown Publishers, 1986), 445.

Chapter 11

1. "Hiroshima: Who's Who and What Did They Say?" www.doug-long.com/quotes for Eisenhower.

2. "Hiroshima: Who's Who and What Did They Say?" www.doug-long.com/quotes for Hoover.

3. Richard B. Frank, *Downfall: The End of the Japanese Empire* (New York, Random House, 1999), 342–43, 351.

4. Thomas M. Coffey, *Iron Eagle: The Turbulent Life of General Curtis LeMay* (New York: Crown Publishers, 1986), 318–19; and William E. Burrows, *By Any Means Necessary: America's Secret Air War in the Cold War* (New York: Farrar, Straus, and Giroux, 2001), 65.

5. Sam Korth, author interview, Mesa, Arizona, September 2005.

6. T. Willard Hunter, *The Spirit of Charles Lindbergh: Another Dimension* (Lanham, MD: Madison Books, Lanham, 1993), 115.

7. James H. Doolittle, author interview, Los Angeles, 1977.

8. Walter J. Boyne, "LeMay," *Air Force* Magazine, March 1998.

Chapter 12

1. Master Sergeant Ken Tomb, USAFR (Ret.) email correspondence with author, October 2005.

2. Master Sergeant Ken Tomb, USAFR (Ret) email correspondence with author, October 2005.

3. "Interview with General Russell E. Dougherty, August 1996." gwu.edu/~nsarchiv/coldwar/interviews/episode–12/dougheit1.html

4. Walter J Boyne, "LeMay." *Air Force Magazine*, Vol. 81, No. 3, March 1998.

5. "Air Force Leadership" www.maxwell.af.mil/au/awc/awcgate/readings/afp35-49-no-cover.pdf

6. Major William H. Allen, USAF (Ret), email correspondence with author, November 21, 2005.

Index

Acknowledgments

Jim Hornfischer; Terry Aitken and Bret Stolle, National Museum of the U.S. Air Force; Major William H. Allen (Ret); Randy Bergeron; Colonel Walter J. Boyne, USAF (Ret); Richard B. Frank; Captain Donald Gordon, USN (Ret); Dr. Richard P. Hallion; Frederick A. Johnsen; Admiral George Kinnear III, USN (Ret); Sam R. Korth; Mark Morgan, Air Mobility Command History Office; Jonathan Parshall; Norman Polmar; M. G. Sheftall; the late Colonel Reade Tilley (Ret); John L. Tillman; Master Sergeant Kenneth S. Tomb, USAFR (Ret).